B

**Amstrad PC's
and
IBM Compatibles**

BOOK 1 – LANGUAGE

ABOUT BOOK – 2

**BP244: BBC BASIC86 on the Amstrad PC's and IBM Compatibles.
Book – 2: Graphics and Disc Files.**

The second book in this series explores the Graphics and Disc Filing capabilities of BBC BASIC86 running on the AMSTRAD PC's and IBM compatibles. It is ideal for those users who would like to be led through the intricacies of graphics, error-handling routines and database filing systems, all of which are illustrated and incorporated into working programs.

BBC BASIC86 on the Amstrad PC's and IBM Compatibles

BOOK 1 — LANGUAGE

by
N. Kantaris and K. Thompson

BERNARD BABANI (publishing) LTD.
THE GRAMPIANS
SHEPHERDS BUSH ROAD
LONDON W6 7NF
ENGLAND

PLEASE NOTE

Although every care has been taken with the production of this book to ensure that any projects, designs, modifications and/or programs etc. contained herewith, operate in a correct and safe manner and also that any components specified are normally available in Great Britain, the Publishers and Author do not accept responsibility in any way for the failure, including fault in design, of any project, design, modification or program to work correctly or to cause damage to any other equipment that it may be connected to or used in conjunction with, or in respect of any other damage or injury that may be so caused, nor do the Publishers accept responsibility in any way for the failure to obtain specified components.

Notice is also given that if equipment that is still under warranty is modified in any way or used or connected with home-built equipment then that warranty may be void.

© 1987 BERNARD BABANI (publishing) LTD

First Published – November 1987

British Library Cataloguing in Publication Data:
  Kantaris, Noel
    BBC Basic86 on the Amstrad PC's and IBM compatibles.
    Bk. 1: Language
    1. BASIC86 (Computer program language)
    I. Title II. Thompson, Keith
    005.2'6   QA76.73.B/

ISBN 0 85934 188 7

Printed and Bound in Great Britain by Cox & Wyman Ltd., Reading

PREFACE

This book is aimed at users of IBM and compatible microcomputers (including the AMSTRAD 1512 and 1640) who want to use BBC-BASIC86. The book is the first of two and deals with the BBC-BASIC86 language; the second book deals with the BBC-BASIC86 Graphics and File handling techniques.

BBC-BASIC introduced on the BBC microcomputer was a great advance on traditional Basic languages. It allowed structured programming to be employed using PROCedures to design modular programs. Throughout the education world BBC-BASIC has become the standard programming language. It has now been developed for the IBM PC and compatible micros as BBC-BASIC86. The Basic interpreter is available on disk from M-TEC, Ollands Road, Reepham, Norfolk; a run-time only version allows programs written in BBC-BASIC86 to be run in computers without the presence of the interpreter.

The book introduces the newcomer to the BBC-BASIC86 language and does not presuppose any prior knowledge of programming. BBC-BASIC statements are introduced and explained with the help of simple programs. The user is encouraged to type these into the computer, save them, and keep improving them as more complex language statements and commands are encountered. This enables the user to build up a considerable library of programs and PROCedures which can become the building blocks of advanced programming techniques.

Graded problems are included in the book together with full working solutions. These solutions and all the programs given in the text can be purchased on disk by writing to the authors at the Camborne School of Mines, Pool, Redruth, Cornwall. Other appendices deal with binary and hexadecimal arithmetic and debugging techniques.

NOTE: The Publishers of this book are in no way responsible for the manufacture or supply of this disk and any enquiries must be sent to the address supplied.

ACKNOWLEDGEMENT: The authors would like to thank Jane Thompson for verifying every single program listing given in this book.

ABOUT THE AUTHORS

N. Kantaris
Graduated in 1959 in Electrical Engineering at Bristol University. Spent three years in the Electronics Industry in London. Appointed as Tutor/Senior Tutor in Physics at the University of Queensland from 1963 to 1971. During this time carried out research leading to an M.E. in Electronics (1968) and a Ph.D in Physics (1972). Appointed as Post-Doctoral Research Fellow in Radio Physics at the University of Leicester until 1973. Appointed as Senior Lecturer in Engineering at The Camborne School of Mines in Cornwall and since 1978 has assumed the responsibility of Head of Computing.

K. Thompson
Graduated in Mining Engineering in 1964 and spent eight years in the mining industry at home and abroad. From 1972-1974 worked in computing and operational research for a large international mining company. In 1974 joined Camborne School of Mines as Head of Management. Currently he is Head of Mining Engineering at the school. Whilst at Cambourne he has been involved with the use of computing and computer simulation techniques in management and mining.

LIST OF CONTENTS

Introduction
- Special keyboard keys requiring attention 1
- Modes of operation 2
- Starting BBC-BASIC 2
- Disk-file handling commands 4
- Using the printer 5
- VDU codes 6

Chapter 1
USING BASIC
- Immediate mode 7
- Deferred mode 8
- Assigning values to variables 9
- Variables, constants and expressions 9
- Entering a new program 12
- The formatted PRINT statement 13
- Problem 1.1 14
- The INPUT statement 15
- Problem 1.2 16
- The READ and DATA statements 16
- Problem 1.3 17
- The RESTORE statement 17
- Priority in arithmetic operations 18
- Table 1.1 Arithmetic Operators and their Priority 19
- Problem 1.4 20

Chapter 2
CONTROL OF PROGRAM FLOW
- The REPEAT-UNTIL Loop 21
- The IF and GOTO statements 21
- Logical operators within an IF statement 23
- Table 2.1 Logical Operators 23
- The IF ... THEN ... ELSE statement 23
- Simple data sorting 24
- Problem 2.1 25
- The computed GOTO statement 25
- Problem 2.2 26
- The FOR-NEXT loop 26
- Use of STEP 28
- Nested FOR-NEXT loops 29
- Problem 2.3 30
- Fig. 2.1 Some loop configurations 30
- Use of FOR-NEXT loops in simple graphics 31
- Problem 2.4 32

Chapter 3
STRINGS AND ARRAYS
String variables	35
Table 3.1 ASCII Conversion Codes	36
String arrays	37
String functions	38
Problem 3.1	41
Subscripted numeric variables	41
Problem 3.2	44
Some more string functions	44
String concatenation	45
Problem 3.3	47
Alphabetical sorting	47
The bubble sort technique	50
Sending output to a printer	51
Problem 3.4	52

Chapter 4
SUBPROGRAMS
Standard arithmetic functions	53
Table 4.1 Standard BASIC Functions	53
SIN(X), COS(X) and TAN(X)	54
ASN(X), ACS(X) and ATN(X)	54
SQR(X)	54
EXP(X)	55
LOG(X) and LN(X)	55
ABS(X)	55
SGN(X)	55
INT(X)	55
RND(X)	56
Derived mathematical functions	58
Table 4.2 Derived mathematical functions	58
User-defined functions	58
Problem 4.1	61
Procedures	61
Fig. 4.1 Diagrammatic representation of program with procedure	62
Right-justifying numbers	64
Problem 4.2	65
Nested procedures	67
Fig. 4.2 Diagrammatic representation of nested procedure	67
Recursion	68
Fig. 4.3 Flow of logic in recursive procedures	69
Subroutines	70
The GOSUB and RETURN Statements	70

Appendix A
 Debugging techniques 73
  Syntax errors 73
  Logic errors 74
  Common causes of errors 76

Appendix B
 Representation of numeric data 77
  Binary representation 77
  Hexadecimal representation 78

Appendix C
 Print formatting 81
  Changing format: The @% variable 81

Solutions to Problems 85

Index 93

TRADE MARKS

IBM is a registered trademark of International Business Machines Corporation

AMSTRAD is a registered trademark of Amstrad Consumer Electronics plc.

Introduction

IBM PC and compatible micros are powerful personal computers. They can use BBC-BASIC86 as their programming language with the advantage of being able to handle much larger programs than the BBC computer as a result of their vastly increased memory. Most programs written for the BBC computer will run on these computers. The BBC computer is supplied with BASIC in a 16 Kbyte ROM chip (this stands for Read-Only-Memory), while the IBM and compatibles require you to purchase the BBC-BASIC86 interpreter on disk. All programs in this book will run on IBM PC compatible and BBC computers.

Special keyboard keys requiring attention

Most computer keyboards can produce all 128 ASCII (American National Standard Code for Information Interchange) character codes, have auto-repeat on all keys and include a full set of cursor-control keys. With the 'SHIFT' key pressed down, capital letters (upper case) will be produced when pressing keys A-Z. Other keys which have two symbols on them will produce the upper of the two symbols.

The CTRL (control) and ALT keys are like extra shift keys giving more possible 'meanings' to each key. BBC-BASIC86 does not use the ALT key because it does not appear on the BBC computer keyboard.

Some special CTRL commands used by BBC-BASIC86, which you will eventually find useful, are listed below. For ease of reading, single quotes will now be used to enclose special keys that the user is required to press. Therefore, 'CTRL'C means press the CTRL key and while continuing to hold it down, press the C key.

'CTRL'SHIFT	Interrupts a program and stops the printing of output on the screen. To continue printing, release the SHIFT key.
'CTRL'N	Prints output on screen one page at a time. Press the SHIFT key to print the next page.
'CTRL'O	Cancels the effect of 'CTRL'N.
'CTRL'B	Connects the computer to the printer.
'CTRL'C	Disconnects the computer from the printer.

Finally, the RETURN and ESCape keys are very important. The RETURN key is pressed to show that a complete instruction to the computer has been typed and the user requires the computer's response. It also has the effect of returning the cursor to the screen's left-hand edge on the following line. Again, to facilitate reading we shall use 'RETURN' to mean 'press the RETURN key'. At the top left of the keyboard there is a key marked ESCape which is used to 'escape' from a program. It is the 'abort' button.

Modes of operation

BBC-BASIC86 emulates MODEs 0-6 of the BBC micro. MODE 7 is only available with the monochrome display adaptor. When you first activate BBC-BASIC it is in MODE 3. To obtain any of the other modes, type

MODE n   (followed by 'RETURN')

where n is the desired mode number. Note that BBC-BASIC86 only recognises commands and BASIC statements typed in upper case.

The modes available in BBC-BASIC are listed below together with the corresponding number of pixels (plotting points on the screen), the number of colours and characters per line on the screen.

MODE	Pixels	No. of Colours	Characters × Lines
0	640×200	2	80×25
1	320×200	4	40×25
2	320×200	4	40×25
3	None	16 Text only	80×25
4	320×200	4	40×25
5	320×200	4	40×25
6	None	16 Text only	40×25
7	None	Monochrome	80×25

Any differences between the characteristics of the above modes and those of the BBC computer are due to hardware differences between BBC and IBM PC compatible computers.

Starting BBC-BASIC

Start BBC-BASIC by putting the BBC-BASIC86 disk in the currently selected drive and typing BBCBASIC.

Now type each line of the following short BASIC program into your computer as it stands, starting with the line numbers and ending each line by pressing the RETURN key.

```
10 PRINT "THIS IS MY FIRST PROGRAM"
20 END
```

If you type something wrong and you discover it before you press the RETURN key, use the BACK SPACE key on the IBM and compatibles (equivalent to the DELETE key on the BBC) to delete the characters to the left of the current cursor position until you have deleted the character in error. Then type the correct character and complete the line. If you discover the error after pressing the RETURN key, then either retype the entire line (if it is a short one), starting with the line number, or use the Editor which is evoked by typing

    *EDIT   (followed by 'RETURN')

The display screen is then cleared and the program is listed with the cursor appearing under the first character following the line number of the first statement. The cursor keys can then be used to position the cursor under the offending character. Typing characters on the keyboard when the cursor is in that position inserts characters into the line, while pressing the DELete key removes the character above the current cursor position. If the INSert key has been pressed, characters typed overwrite the characters on the screen. You only need to correct the incorrect characters and then exit the Editor by pressing the ESCape key.

To run (execute) the program, type

    RUN   (followed by 'RETURN')

If the program was typed in correctly the message

    THIS IS MY FIRST PROGRAM

will appear on the screen. If instead you get the message

    Mistake on line n

where n is a number, then you must have made a mistake when typing the mentioned line and the computer does not understand your instructions. If that is the case, retype or edit (as instructed above) the offending line and then type RUN again.

When all is well, type

    SAVE "MYFIRST"   (followed by 'RETURN')

where MYFIRST is the name which we have chosen to call the program. The program, now in the computer's memory, will be SAVEd on the disk under the filename MYFIRST. The abreviation SA. (for SAVE) can be used.

A filename must not be longer than eight characters. If it is, it will be truncated to eight characters. To be safe use only letters or letters and numbers. Such files will be SAVEd with the three letter extention BBC. When you catalogue the disc, the directory will be displayed with the filenames followed by a dot and the extension BBC.

Now type

    *   (followed by 'RETURN')

The disk drive will operate and amongst the filenames displayed on the screen will be the name of the program you have just SAVEd. Now type

        LIST   (followed by 'RETURN')

As long as the program is in memory, BASIC will list it. The abreviation L. (for LIST) can be used. If the program is eventually erased from memory (one way of doing this is by typing NEW), it can be re-LOADed from the disk by typing

        LOAD "MYFIRST"   (followed by 'RETURN')

This is the last time we shall remind you to press RETURN after typing a statement or command. The LOAD command, once executed, replaces any program currently in the computer's memory by the newly LOADed program. The abreviation LO. (for LOAD) can be used.

Disk-file handling commands

A BBC-BASIC program can be removed from the disk by typing the DELete command

        *DEL "filename"

where "filename" is the actual name of the file you want to DELete. This can be verified by typing *. after the drive has stopped operating. To illustrate this point, LOAD the MYFIRST program and then SAVE it under the filename TEST. On typing *. two file names will appear on the disk's directory. The file called TEST is a copy of the file called MYFIRST. We can now experiment with the TEST file without any fear that we might lose the MYFIRST program from the disk.

The Disk Operating System allows us to carry out many housekeeping operations with the saved files. One such operation is to REName an existing file. To do this, type

        *REN TEST MYPROG

You will now find on the disk's directory that the file name TEST has been replaced by the file name MYPROG.

To DELete a file, type

        *DEL MYPROG

The available Operating System commands are listed below.

*.	Displays the files on the disk directory.
*DEL filename	Deletes the specified filename from the disk's directory
*DIR	Displays the disk's directory.
*DRIVE	Allows you to change the currently logged disk drive. For example, *DRIVE B: (or *DR. B: for short) changes the logged drive to B:.
*EXEC filename	Provides input from the specified text (ASCII) file, as if the information was typed on the keyboard.
*HELP	Displays the BBC-BASIC86 Version number
*KEY n	Programs the specified user-defined function key. For example, *KEY 1 RUN defines function key 1 to type the command RUN. To include the 'RETURN' in the definition, type *KEY 1 RUN|M.
*RENAME	Renames a filename on disk.
*SPOOL filename	Saves all text subsequently displayed on screen by the LIST command into the specified text (ASCII) file. To close the file, type *SPOOL (without the filename) after the LIST command has been executed.

From within BBC-BASIC all MS-DOS commands can be accessed by prefixing them with a double asterisk. For example, **DIR will display the DOS directory.

Using the printer

As programs become longer than the 25 lines normally available on your display screen, it helps to be able to obtain a hardcopy (a copy on paper) of the program listing. To do this, the following procedure must be followed.

(i) Load the program into memory, unless it is already there, by typing

LOAD "filename"

(ii) Type the command (with printer switched on)

'CTRL'B   or   VDU2

(iii) Type

LIST

On pressing the RETURN key the program will be LISTed on paper.

(iv) When printing has finished, type the command

'CTRL'C   or   VDU3

which will disconnect the printer.

Try the above procedure using the MYFIRST program.

For the sake of completeness, the BBC-BASIC86 VDU codes are listed below together with their meaning.

CODE	MEANING
0	Null – does nothing
1	Sends the next character to the printer only
2	Enables the printer
3	Disables the printer
4	Writes text at the text cursor position
5	Writes text at the graphics cursor position
6	Enables output to the screen
7	Bell – makes the speaker beep
8	Moves cursor backwards one character
9	Moves the text cursor forwards one character
10	Moves the text cursor down one line
11	Moves the text cursor up one line
12	Clears the text area – as does CLS
13	Moves the text cursor to the start of the current line
14	Enables the auto-paging mode
15	Disables the auto-paging mode
16	Clears the graphics area – as does CLG
17	Defines a text colour – as does COLOUR
18	Defines a graphics colour – as does GCOL
19	Selects a colour palette
20	Restores the default logical colours
21	Disables output to the screen
22	Selects the screen mode – as does MODE
23	Programs characters and controls the cursor
24	Defines a graphics window
25	Plots to the screen – as does PLOT
26	Restores the default text and graphics windows
27	Sends the next character to the screen
28	Defines a text window
29	Sets the graphics origin
30	Sends the text cursor to the top left corner of the screen
31	Moves the text cursor – as does TAB(X,Y)
127	Backspace and delete.

Chapter 1

Using BASIC

Unless otherwise specified, BASIC in this book refers to the BASIC language implemented on the BBC, IBM and compatible computers. It is often referred to as BBC-BASIC as it was used first on the BBC microcomputer.

Immediate mode

Computers can be used in immediate mode, that is, not with a program, to perform arithmetic. To illustrate this, type

    PRINT 15+5   (and don't forget to press RETURN)

BASIC will respond by writing

    20

If instead the message Mistake appears on the screen you must have made a mistake when typing the statement. Try another, by typing

    PRINT 25−14

BASIC will respond by writing

    11

Now type

    PRINT 25*3

BASIC will write

    75

Note that the asterisk (*) is the special character for multiplication. No other character can be used to indicate this arithmetic operation. Now type

    PRINT 15/3

BASIC will write

    5

Again note that the stroke (/) is the special character for division and that no other character can be used as an alternative for this operation. Now type

    PRINT 2^3

BASIC will write

   8

Note that this symbol (^) stands for 'raise to the power of', and the above statement is interpreted as 'raise 2 to the power of 3' (that is 2×2×2). Again, the character (^) is the only character that can be used to indicate this type of mathematical operation.

Deferred mode

In the previous section, statements such as PRINT were executed immediately the RETURN key was pressed. There is, however, another way in which BASIC statements can be written so that their execution is deferred until the command RUN, followed by 'RETURN' is typed. Note that all commands should be followed by 'RETURN'.

Deferred mode statements must be preceded by a number, referred to as the line number, which must be an integer (whole number) in the range 1 to 65535. To allow later insertion of new lines, it is advisable to number lines in tens. Type the following statements, remembering to press the RETURN key at the end of each line.

     10 PRINT 5*2-2
     20 PRINT 30/2+5
     30 END

This is a program. The statement of line 30 tells BASIC that it is the end of the program, and execution will terminate at that point. Now type the command

     RUN

BASIC will write

     8   20

with eight spaces in front of the first number. Numbers are printed right-justified in a nine character wide area of the screen, called a field.

Now, suppose we wanted to know not only the individual result of lines 10 and 20, but also their sum. We could achieve this by inserting into the program the statement

     25 PRINT (5*2-2)+(30/2+5)

After typing the above line, type the command

     LIST

BASIC will respond by listing the program in memory, in ascending line number order, with line 25 in the correct place. Now type

RUN

BASIC will respond by writing

     8   20   28

which indicates that the program statements were also executed in ascending line number order.

Assigning values to variables

Line 25 of the previous program is to some extent a repetition of lines 10 and 20. A better method of writing this program would be to assign the values of the expressions of lines 10 and 20 to two different variable names and then PRINT out the values of the variables. For example,

```
 5 A=5*2-2
10 PRINT A
15 B=30/2+5
20 PRINT B
25 PRINT A+B
```

If you LIST the program you will see that the old lines, which had the same line numbers as the ones just typed in, have been replaced by the new entries, but line 30 is still there. If you now RUN the program, BASIC will respond by writing the same answers as before. Now type

     25   (followed by 'RETURN')

On LISTing the program, you will see that line 25 has been removed from the program and can only be re-inserted by retyping it. With this method, unwanted lines can be removed from a BASIC program.

Variables, constants and expressions

Variables

A variable is a symbol which represents a number. In some versions of BASIC a variable is formed by either a single letter or by a letter followed by another letter or a single digit number. Examples of permissible variables in such versions of BASIC are

    A, AA, AZ, A1, A9

with all letters being in upper case (capitals).

With BBC-BASIC, variable names may be much longer, longer than you would ever need, but you must be careful not to use a variable name which starts with a BASIC reserved word such as

DRAW FOR IF NEXT ON OR TO

to mention but a few. A full list of all BASIC reserved words for these computers are to be found in the appropriate 'User Guide'.

To overcome errors caused by the use of such variable names, we will adopt the convention of having the first letter of long variable names in capitals, the rest being in lower case. Yes! BBC-BASIC allows the use of lower case, upper case and a mixture of the two when writing variable names. The only restrictions are that the first character of a variable name must be a letter and spaces or special characters must not be used. For example,

    Draw, Forest, One, Tone

are acceptable variable names. They are treated totally differently from

    DRAW, FOREST, ONE, TONE

all of which are either straightforward BASIC commands (such as DRAW) or start with BASIC reserved words (such as FORest, ONe and TOne – the reserved words in capitals for clarity).

We shall only use long variable names when they help you to understand what the program is doing. It is often better, for example, to use X and Y rather than Xvalue and Yvalue, particularly if such variables are typed many times and you are a one-finger typist!

Constants
BASIC accepts constants expressed in either integer, decimal or exponential form. Hexadecimal notation can also be used (Appendix C). For example,

    255   is an integer number
    26.75   is a decimal (or floating point) number
    2.368E9 is an exponential number. The E here can be read as 'times ten to the power of'.

Results of computations are printed out in integer or decimal form when the number will fit into nine characters. Outside this range, when computations result in very large or very small numbers, they are printed in exponential format. For example, a number such as 2369000000 will be printed as 2.369E9 and 0.00000005126 as 5.126E-8.

Real and Integer variables

The variables we have discussed so far are known as 'real' variables which can hold 'real' or 'floating-point' numbers within the range $+2\times10^{-39}$ to $+2\times10^{+38}$. Such variables are only stored to 9 figure accuracy.

For greater accuracy, 'integer' variables must be used. These are distinguished from real variables by the addition of the % sign at the end of their name. Thus, the variable name Number is a real variable and can hold real numbers, while the variable name Number% is an integer variable which can hold integer numbers within the range -2,147,483,648 to 2,147,483,647. Integer numbers in this range are held by integer variables with absolute accuracy and results of arithmetic calculations, which are performed much faster than equivalent real number calculations, are very accurate. However, be warned that integer arithmetic may give unexpected results. Integer division will not give the same results as real number division because integer variables do not contain decimal points. Dividing integer 10 by integer 3 will give the answer 3. The remainder is lost. In the same way integer 10 divided by integer 11 is 0!

There are two operators which are useful when performing integer division. These are the DIV and the MOD. The DIV operator gives the whole number part of the result of a division, while the MOD operator gives the remainder. For example, typing

    PRINT 10 DIV 3

gives the result 3, while typing

    PRINT 10 MOD 3

gives the result 1.

It must be stressed however that the numbers on which DIV and MOD operate (called the operands) are first converted to integers. Thus, the same results would be obtained from the above operations if number 10 above was 10.1 or 10.9 and number 3 was 3.1 or 3.9.

The 26, single-letter, integer variables A% to Z% are special variables called 'resident integer variables'. They are the only variables that do not lose their value between programs provided you haven't exited from BBC-BASIC or switched the computer off. If any of these variables are assigned values in one program, they retain them and can be used in programs run later.

Expressions

An expression, when referred to in this text, implies a constant, a variable or a combination of either or both, separated by arithmetic or logical operators.

Entering a new program

To enter a new program into the computer, type the command

    NEW

The command NEW erases programs currently held in memory. Type LIST to check this. The computer is ready to accept a new program. If you did not really mean to erase the program from memory, BBC-BASIC allows you to retrieve the NEWly erased program by typing the command

    OLD

before you type anything else. If you type anything other than OLD the program will be lost. The abreviation O. (for OLD) can be used. Try these commands and use the LIST command to verify what is happening.

The following program assigns values to three variables and then calculates and prints their average value.

```
10 REM AVERAGES
20 A=26.9
30 B=28.2
40 C=27.3
50 PRINT A,B,C
60 D=A+B+C
70 X=D/3
80 PRINT "AVERAGE=";X
90 END
```

On RUNning the program, BASIC will respond by writing

        26.9   28.2   27.3
AVERAGE=27.4666667

on the screen.

There are a few unfamiliar statements introduced in this program which need to be explained. Line 10 is a REM (Remark) statement which allows the user to insert notes and comments in a program. Remarks throughout the body of a long program help the programmer to remember the function of various program sections. REM statements have no effect on the running of the program, but they do take up memory space.

Line 50 has all three variables in a PRINT statement, separated by commas. This causes the values of these variables to be displayed on the same line, right-justified in fields of 10 characters. Since there is room for 80 characters on each line of your monitor screen in this mode (other modes will be discussed later), you can print a maximum of eight numbers per line. If the three variables A, B and C are separated by semicolons, BASIC writes their value close together without any intervening spaces. Try it by re-typing line 50 and RUNning the program.

Line 80 has a set of characters (AVERAGE=) enclosed in double quotation marks (called a string). The PRINT has the effect of displaying the actual characters which are enclosed in the quotation marks exactly as they appear in the statement. It is a way of providing captions or headings for the computer's output.

Formatted PRINT statement

Presentation of results can be made very much easier to understand by using the PRINT TAB statement which allows output to be displayed in columns. There are 80 tabulation positions on each of the 24 lines available on your screen. The program below illustrates the use of this statement.

```
10 REM USE OF PRINT TAB
20 A=15
30 B=25
40 C=10
50 D=20
60 PRINT TAB(5);"A";TAB(10);"B";TAB(15);"C";
   TAB(20);"D"
70 PRINT TAB(5);A;TAB(10);B;TAB(15);C;TAB(20);D
80 END
```

On RUNning this program BASIC will respond by writing

```
A         B         C         D
15        25        10        20
```

Had we wanted to tabulate the above information in the four default columns available when using commas to separate variable names, we would write lines 60 and 70 as follows:

```
60 PRINT "A","B","C","D"
70 PRINT TAB(0);A;TAB(10);B;TAB(20);C;TAB(30);D
```

Strings of characters are PRINTed left-justified so by including the TAB statements in line 70, we force the computer to output the numeric information at the beginning of the first four preformatted columns on the screen, thus lining up the numbers under the respective strings.

Another formatting function is the PRINT SPC statement which provides a number of spaces between the last printed position and the next one. For example, line 60 of the above program can be replaced by

```
60 PRINT SPC(5);"A";SPC(4);"B";SPC(4);"C";SPC(4);"D"
```

The PRINT TAB or PRINT SPC statements cannot be used to move to the left of a current printing position in a given line. Only progressive moves to the right are obeyed.

―――――――――――――――― **Problem 1.1** ――――――――――――――――
Modify the AVERAGE program by incorporating the PRINT TAB statement so that the output appears in tabular form, under appropriate headings as shown below.

    VALUES: A   B   C   AVERAGE
―――

BBC-BASIC supports one additional tabulation statement, TAB(X,Y) which should be used in conjunction with a PRINT statement. This positions the cursor at any point on the screen, irrespective of its current position. To illustrate its use, clear the screen with the CLS (CLear Screen) command.

The command CLS can be used in either immediate or deferred mode. In both cases it clears the screen and sends the cursor to the upper left-hand corner of the screen. This command, in its deferred mode, is incorporated in the program given below which prints the letter X in the middle of the screen.

```
10 REM USE OF CLS
20 REM AND TAB(X,Y)
30 CLS
40 PRINT TAB(40,12);"X"
50 END
```

Note that in Mode 3 the value of X in the TAB(X,Y) statement should lie between 0 and 79, while that for Y must lie between 0 and 24.

The PRINT TAB(X,Y) statement in the program below places an asterisk at each corner of the monitor's screen. Allowance is made for the appearance of the cursor at the bottom of the screen, after the execution of the program, which has the effect of scrolling the information on the screen upwards by a line.

```
10 REM PLACING ASTERISKS AT CORNERS OF SCREEN
20 CLS
30 PRINT TAB(0,2);"*";
40 PRINT TAB(79,2);"*"
50 PRINT TAB(0,24);"*";
60 PRINT TAB(79,24);"*"
70 END
```

Note that in order to counteract the two-line scroll of information on the screen, we TAB in the Y-direction to position 2 instead of position 0 when placing the asterisks at the top corners of the screen.

The INPUT statement

The INPUT statement is used to enter data from the keyboard. This will be illustrated by writing a program to calculate 15% of any number. The number itself is entered via the INPUT statement as shown below.

```
10 REM PERCENT PROGRAM
20 INPUT Number
30 Rate=15
40 Value=Number*Rate/100
50 PRINT Value
60 END
```

The INPUT statement in line 20 will cause BASIC to halt execution, print a question mark (?) and wait for the user to type in a numerical value. Try it by RUNning the program. When the computer prints the question mark, type 300 (not forgetting the 'RETURN'). BASIC will now execute the remaining statements and will print

45

The program can be made more general by using the INPUT statement in line 30. In this way, any percentage of any number can be calculated. To avoid making mistakes in our responses we can incorporate messages in the INPUT statement. For example, change lines 20 and 30 to the following:

```
20 INPUT "ENTER NUMBER",Number
30 INPUT "ENTER %",Rate
```

On RUNning this program, the computer will write

ENTER NUMBER?

with the cursor positioned after the question mark (BBC-BASIC automatically gives you a ?). If we type 400 (say), the computer will now execute line 30 and will write

ENTER %?

and wait for the numerical entry. Type 10. The computer will execute the rest of the program and will write

40

When a word which is enclosed in double quotes (called a string) is included in an INPUT statement, the question mark printed by the computer can be suppressed by typing a space in place of the comma following the string. Try it.

A better version of the previous program is given below.

```
10 REM GENERAL PERCENT
20 INPUT "ENTER NUMBER " Number
30 INPUT "ENTER % " Rate
40 Value=Number*Rate/100
50 PRINT Rate;" % OF ";Number;" = ";Value
60 END
```

On RUNning the above program and entering the same numeric values for Number and Rate as previously, the computer will write

10 % OF 400 = 40

providing a more meaningful output. Note that each string in the INPUT statement of this program incorporates a space adjacent to the closing quotation marks. This was introduced deliberately to provide a space between the end of the string and the beginning of any numeric entry from the keyboard.

SAVE this program for future use, under the file name PERCENT.

──────────────── **Problem 1.2** ────────────────

Write a program, using the INPUT statement, which can convert degrees Fahrenheit (F) to degrees Celsius (C). Use the relationship

Degrees Celsius=(Degrees Fahrenheit-32)*5/9

───

The READ and DATA statements

In previous examples, constant values were assigned to single variables either within the program or through the use of the INPUT statement; if more variables were needed, more such assignments were made. In programs requiring many variables and constants, especially when they are not expected to change between each RUN, the READ and DATA statements should be used.

The DATA statement introduces a numeric constant, or a series of constants, into a program. The READ statement links variable names sequentially with the constant values supplied by the DATA statement. READ and DATA statements must accompany one another within a program, but they need not be paired. If five variables appear in one or more READ statements, there must be at least five constants in one or more DATA statements.

In the following example, all data is introduced in a single DATA statement. It is used at separate points in the program by two READ statements.

```
10 REM USE OF READ STATEMENT
20 READ A,B
30 X=A+B
40 PRINT A,B,X
50 READ C,D
60 Y=C+D
70 PRINT C,D,Y
80 DATA 1,5,2,6
90 END
```

On RUNning this program, BASIC will respond by writing

```
1       5       6
2       6.      8
```

In executing such a program, BASIC ignores all DATA statements (even if such statements appear on lines preceding the READ statements) until it encounters a READ statement. It then goes back to the lowest numbered statement line of the program and starts to search for a DATA statement. Here it finds one at line 80, the next-to-last line of the program. Taking constant values sequentially, it associates them with variables in the READ statement, also taken sequentially: A is assigned a value of 1, and B a value of 5. After leaving a pointer at the next data element, 2, it reverts to line 30, the next executable statement. On reaching line 50, where another READ statement is encountered, BASIC does not search for the DATA statement, but refers to its pointer to obtain the next unused data element, which is 2. Variables C and D are therefore assigned the constant values 2 and 6.

If the total number of constants in all DATA statements is less than the total number of variables in all READ statements, BASIC will respond with an error message which indicates lack of data. Excess data are ignored.

―――――――――――――――――― **Problem 1.3** ――――――――――――――――――
Write a program, using the READ and DATA statements, which assigns three numbers to the variables Days, Hours and Minutes and then calculates and prints the total number of minutes involved.

―――――――――――――――――――――――――――――――――――――――

The RESTORE statement

The RESTORE statement has no parameters or options. It simply makes it possible to recycle through DATA statements beginning with the lowest numbered DATA line in the program. The following example illustrates its use.

```
10 REM USE OF RESTORE
20 READ A,B
30 PRINT A,B
40 RESTORE
50 READ C,D
60 PRINT C,D
70 DATA 2,7
80 END
```

On RUNning the program BASIC will write

```
2       7
2       7
```

The RESTORE statement at line 40 allows the READ statement at line 50 to obtain values from the DATA statement, even though the same values were used previously in the READ statement of line 20. Without the RESTORE statement, an error message indicating lack of data for the second READ statement would have occurred. The statement merely moves the data list pointer back to the beginning of the data list. It is ignored in programs which do not contain READ and DATA statements.

Priority in arithmetic operations

We shall now examine a modified AVERAGE program, used at the beginning of this chapter, and see how the various arithmetic operations were performed.

```
10 REM AVERAGES WITH READ
20 READ A,B,C
30 D=A+B+C
40 X=D/3
50 PRINT "AVERAGE = ";X
60 DATA 26.9, 28.2, 27.3
70 END
```

The calculations in this program are performed in statements 30 and 40. Combining them into one line, we could write

$X=(A+B+C)/3$ (Not $X=A+B+C/3$)

It is important that the numerator of this expression is in brackets. If it were not, BASIC would evaluate first C/3 and then add to it A+B, which would give the wrong result. This is due to an inbuilt system of priorities (see Table 1.1).

On RUNning the program, BASIC will write

AVERAGE = 27.4666667

on the screen.

TABLE 1.1 Arithmetic Operators and their Priority

BASIC symbol	Example	Priority	Function
( )	(A+B)/N	1	Parenthesized operation
^	A^N	2	Raise A to the Nth power
*	A*N	3	Multiplication
/	A/N	3	Division
+	A+N	4	Addition
−	A-N	4	Subtraction

On evaluating expressions, BASIC performs arithmetical operations in the order of priority indicated in Table 1.1. Expressions in parentheses are evaluated first. Nested groups in parentheses are evaluated beginning with the innermost grouping and working outwards.

BASIC cannot accept two consecutive operators. For example, A*-N is illegal. It must be written as A*(-N). Through the use of parentheses, the order of priority of execution, and therefore the final value of an expression, can be changed. If a line has an expression which contains several operators of equal priority, BASIC will evaluate it from left to right.

Let us examine how a complicated expression such as

$$Y = (A+B*X)^2/C-D*X^3$$

is evaluated. We assume that the values of A, B, C, D and X are known. First the parenthesized portion of the expression will be evaluated. Within these parentheses the multiplication has a higher priority and therefore it will be evaluated first. Then, A will be added to it, resulting in a numerical value to which we will assign the letter Z. Now the expression is reduced to the following:

$$Y=Z^2/C-D*X^3$$

The above has two exponential expressions, the leftmost of which is evaluated first. Writing Z1 for the result of Z^2 and X1 for the result of X^3, the expression is now reduced to

$$Y=Z1/C-D*X1$$

Again, since division and multiplication have the same priority, the leftmost expression is evaluated first. Finally, the result of the multiplication is taken away from the result of the division and assigned to Y.

All this procedure is, of course, carried out automatically by BASIC but if you intend to use complicated mathematical expressions you must be familiar with it.

Note that what appears as an equation above is, in fact, an assignment statement and not an algebraic identity. As long as the values of variables on the right of an equals sign are known, the calculated result will be assigned to the variable on the left of the equals sign. As an example, consider the following lines.

```
10 K=0
20 K=K+1
30 PRINT K
40 END
```

Line 20 would be meaningless had it been an algebraic expression. In computing terms the statement states 'take the present value in K, add one to it and store the result in K'. When line 20 is executed, the value of K (set in line 10) is zero and adding one to it results in a new value of K equal to one. On RUNning this program, BASIC will write

1

on the screen.

---------------- Problem 1.4 ----------------

In each of the following expressions, the variables used have the following values:

Variable	A	B	C	D	E	F	G
Value	5	3	8	4	7	2	6

Use your computer in immediate mode to work out the correct answer to the expressions given below. To arrive at the final answer, calculate all intermediate steps in the order dictated by the priority procedure.

```
X1=A*B^E+F
X2=A*B^(E+F)
X3=A*B/C*D
X4=A*B/(C*D)
X5=A+B*G+C*G^2+D*G^3
X6=(A+B)*G+C*G^2+D*G^3
X7=(A^F+(B-1/C)^F)^0.5
X8=(A^F+B-1/C^F)^0.5
X9=A/B^2-C*D/((E+F)+G^3)
```

To check your answers, write a program which assigns values to A, B, C etc., and then solves the expressions for X1, X2, X3 etc.

Chapter 2
Control of Program Flow

The REPEAT-UNTIL loop
The REPEAT and UNTIL statements provide a method of looping through statements. The REPEAT marks the beginning of the loop, while the UNTIL marks the end. Any statements between the REPEAT and its corresponding UNTIL will be executed repeatedly until the trailer of the UNTIL statements is true. To illustrate the use of these loop statements, LOAD the PERCENT program and add lines 15 and 55, as shown below.

```
10 REM GENERAL PERCENT
15 REPEAT
20   INPUT "ENTER NUMBER " Number
30   INPUT "ENTER % " Rate
40   Value=Number*Rate/100
50   PRINT Rate;" % OF ";Number;" = ";Value:PRINT
55 UNTIL Number<1
60 END
```

All statements between lines 15 and 55 are REPEATed UNTIL the trailer of UNTIL is true (that is, until you type 0 (zero) or a negative value). Note however, that when you type either 0 (zero) or a negative number you are still asked to ENTER % which shows that the statements between the REPEAT-UNTIL loop are being executed until the end of the loop is reached.

The IF and GOTO statements
The IF statement allows conditional program branching. To illustrate the point, add line 25 (given below) to the PERCENT program. Type

```
25 IF Number<1 THEN GOTO 60
```

and re-RUN the program. If you now want to stop execution simply type 0 (zero) after 'ENTER NUMBER' appears on the screen. When BASIC encounters this IF statement, it compares the value of the variable Number with the constant appearing after the logical operator (in this case the less sign). If the test condition is met, the trailer of the IF statement is executed (in this case transferring control to line 60). If, however, the test condition is not met, the next sequentially numbered statement after the IF statement is executed (in this case line 30).

A better variation of the IF statement would be

```
25 IF Number<1 THEN END
```

which avoids the use of the GOTO statement. Note the use of THEN; it is used prior to introducing another BASIC statement in the trailer of the IF statement. The last modification to line 25 makes line 60 in the program superfluous and it can therefore be deleted. Also note that with these modifications we have made the trailer of the UNTIL statement redundant; it merely acts as a device to force looping. In such cases there is a better trailer we could use, namely FALSE. Thus line 55 now becomes

    55 UNTIL FALSE

which will cause repeated looping. The counterpart of FALSE is TRUE which if used in this program would terminate the program after the first loop.

Finally, to allow a blank line to appear between successive executions of the program, type

    52 PRINT

When BASIC encounters this line it simply prints a space and skips to the next line on the screen. It is said to produce a 'line feed', this being a term used originally when talking about computer printers.

Make all of these changes, and SAVE the program under the original filename PERCENT, re-LOAD and LIST it. You should now have the following program on the screen

```
10 REM GENERAL PERCENT
15 REPEAT
20    INPUT "ENTER NUMBER " Number
25    IF Number<1 THEN END
30    INPUT "ENTER % " Rate
40    Value=Number*Rate/100
50    PRINT Rate;" % OF ";Number;" = ";Value
52    PRINT
55 UNTIL FALSE
```

Logical operators within IF statements
The table below shows all the logical operators allowed within an IF statement.

TABLE 2.1 Logical Operators

BASIC symbol	Example	Meaning
=	A = B	A equal to B
<	A < B	A less than B
<=	A <= B	A less than or equal to B
>	A > B	A greater than B
>=	A >= B	A greater than or equal to B
<>	A <> B	A not equal to B

The IF ... THEN ... ELSE statement
In many cases we have to perform an IF statement twice over to detect which of two similar conditions is true. This is illustrated below.

```
10 REM TWO IF STATEMENTS
20 REPEAT
30   INPUT "ENTER A NUMBER WITHIN 1 TO 99 " N
40   IF N<10 THEN PRINT "ONE DIGIT NUMBER"
50   IF N>9 THEN PRINT "TWO DIGIT NUMBER"
60 UNTIL N<1
```

A more advanced version of the IF statement allows both actions to be inserted in its trailer. An example of this is incorporated in the modified program below.

```
10 REM USE OF IF ... THEN ... ELSE
20 REPEAT
30   INPUT "ENTER A NUMBER WITHIN 1 TO 99 " N
40   IF N<10 THEN PRINT "ONE DIGIT NUMBER" ELSE
     PRINT "TWO DIGIT NUMBER"
50 UNTIL N<1
```

RUN the program and supply numbers between 1 and 99. Obviously, if you type in numbers greater than 99 the program will not function correctly in its present form. But assuming that you have obeyed the message and typed 50 the second BASIC statement in the trailer of the IF statement (after the ELSE) will be executed. If the number entered was less than 10, the first BASIC statement after THEN would be executed. To stop the programs enter a 0 (zero) or a negative value.

Simple data sorting

The program below allows us to enter two numbers, tests to find out which is the larger of the two and prints them in descending order.

```
10 REM TWO NUMBER SORT
20 REPEAT
30    INPUT A,B
40    IF A<0 THEN END
50    IF A>=B THEN PRINT A,B ELSE PRINT B,A
60 UNTIL FALSE
```

The program can be stopped by entering a negative value for A. Otherwise, A is compared with B and the appropriate PRINT statement in the trailer of the IF statement is executed.

The sorting problem becomes more complicated, however, if instead of two numbers we introduce a third one. For two number sorting we had two possible PRINT statements (the number of possible permutations being 1*2=2). For three number sorting however, the total number of PRINT statements becomes six (the number of possible permutations being equal to 1*2*3=6). The combinations are (A,B,C), (A,C,B), (C,A,B), (C,B,A), (B,C,A) and (B,A,C).

A slight variation of the IF statement reduces the total number of statements required to solve this problem. We can, for example, ask whether A is greater than B and B greater than C in one statement, thus combining two statements into one. This form of IF statement is:

IF A>B AND B>C THEN PRINT A,B,C

The trailer of this IF statement will only be executed if, and only if, both A is greater than B and also B is greater than C.

There is another combination of the IF statement which is useful. This is:

IF A>B OR B>C THEN PRINT A,B,C

Returning to the problem of sorting three numbers, if we were to pursue the suggested method, we would require five IF statements to PRINT six combinations of A,B,C. The logic suggested in dealing with the problem would result in a very inefficient program.

Here is a way in which, with only two IF statements and one PRINT statement, the same solution to the three-number sorting problem can be achieved. It uses a different logic and it is explained here with the help of three imaginary playing cards. Assume that you are holding these cards in your hand and you wish to arrange them in descending order. Look at the front two and arrange them so that the highest value appears in front. Now look at the back two and arrange them so that the highest of these two is now in front. Obviously, if the highest card had been at the back, in the first instance, it would by now have moved to the middle position, so a repeat of the whole procedure is necessary to ensure that the highest card is at the front.

We can now write the program to achieve this solution. Note that we use the capability of BASIC to accept multiple statements on one line, provided we separate them with a colon (:). This allows for shorter code and avoids too many GOTO statements which will otherwise have to be used.

```
10 REM THREE NUMBER SORT
20 INPUT A,B,C
30 IF A<B THEN T=A:A=B:B=T
40 IF B<C THEN T=B:B=C:C=T:GOTO 30
50 PRINT A,B,C
60 END
```

Type this program and SAVE it under the file name NRSORT. The following actions are indicated: If the value in A is less than that in B, exchange them so that the value of A is now stored in B and the value of B is now stored in A. Note, however, that were we to put the value of B into A, we should lose the number stored in A (by overwriting). We therefore transfer the contents of A to a temporary variable T, then transfer the contents of B to A and finally transfer the contents of T to B. The second rotation, necessary when B is less than C, is achieved in a similar manner.

——————————————— Problem 2.1 ———————————————
Modify the NRSORT program so that it incorporates the REPEAT-UNTIL loop to allow repeated execution of the program. Also provide a method of stopping execution.

The computed GOTO statement
This is a statement which allows you to divert the execution of your program to one of several lines. The statement is written as follows:

ON X GOTO 100,200,300

The value of X can be an integer constant or an expression. When BASIC encounters the ON ... GOTO, it works out the value of X and if it is equal to 1, it branches to the first line number given in the trailer of the statement (in this case line 100); when X is equal to 2, it branches to the second (in this case line 200), and so on. If X has a value less than 1 or greater than the total number of line numbers in the trailer of the statement, BASIC issues an 'ON range' error.

As an example, consider the program below which can find either the square root, the square or the cube of any number.

```
10 REM USE OF ON-GOTO
20 REPEAT:PRINT
30     INPUT "NUMBER PLEASE " N
40     INPUT "Squareroot/Square/Cube/END (1/2/3/4) " K
50     ON K GOTO 70,100,130,60
60     END
70     Squareroot=N^0.5
80     PRINT "THE SQUARE ROOT OF ";N;" = ";Squareroot
90     UNTIL FALSE
100 Square=N^2
110 PRINT "THE SQUARE OF ";N;" = ";Square
120 UNTIL FALSE
130 Cube=N^3
140 PRINT "THE CUBE OF ";N;" = ";Cube
150 UNTIL FALSE
```

To stop this program type 4 in response to the second INPUT statement.

Note: Because of the way a computer holds numbers in its memory, the square root of 81 is evaluated as 9.0000001.

---------------- **Problem 2.2** ----------------

Write a program that can carry out any of the following conversions:

(a) gallons into litres   (1 gallon = 4.54609 litres)
(b) feet into metres   (1 foot = 0.3048 metres)
(c) pounds into kilograms   (1 pound = 0.453592 kilogram)

Use READ and DATA statements to enter the conversion constants into the computer, and the INPUT statement for entering the number to be converted and the type of conversion required.

The FOR-NEXT loop

The FOR and NEXT statements are used to mark the beginning and ending points of program loops. Any statements between the FOR and its corresponding NEXT will be executed repeatedly according to the conditions supplied by the 'control variable' within the FOR statement. An example follows.

```
10 REM USE OF FOR-NEXT LOOP
20 FOR K=1 TO 5 STEP 1
30     PRINT K
40 NEXT K
50 END
```

In line 20, the control variable K is assigned the value 1 which is increased repeatedly by the number following STEP until it reaches 5. It thus has the values 1, 2, 3, 4 and 5. Since it cannot have these values simultaneously, a loop is formed beginning with the FOR at line 20 and ending with the NEXT at line 40. The statements within the loop are re-executed five times, each time with a new value for K. The NEXT statement increases the value of K and causes repeated jumps to line 20 until K exceeds its final assigned value of 5. When this happens, control passes to whatever statement follows the NEXT statement (in this case line 50).

The FOR-NEXT loop replaces the need for the initialisation, testing and incrementing of the counter K in the following program, which is equivalent to the preceding one:

```
10 REM ACCUMULATOR
20 K=1
30 REPEAT
40     PRINT K
50     K=K+1
60 UNTIL K>5
70 END
```

Line 20 and part of 60 of this program achieve the same as line 20 of the previous one, while line 50 and a different part of 60 have the same function as that of line 40 of the previous program. Note the form of the statement in line 50 of the latest program. On execution, it adds one to the old value of K and stores the result in variable K. It can, therefore, be thought of as an accumulator. On RUNning the program, BASIC will print the values 1, 2, 3, 4 and 5.

The following program makes use of the FOR-NEXT loop as well as an accumulator to find the sum of a list of numbers

```
10 REM SUM OF N NUMBERS
20 READ N
30 Sum=0
40 FOR I=1 TO N STEP 1
50     READ Value
60     Sum=Sum+Value
70 NEXT I
80 PRINT "SUM OF ";N;" NUMBERS = ";Sum
90 DATA 5,20.5,21.3,20.8,20.6,21.1
100 END
```

On RUNning this program, N is assigned the value 5 which is the total number of entries requiring summation. The accumulator Sum is then zeroed in line 30, and a FOR-NEXT loop is set up between lines 40 and 70. Note that the limits of the control variable in the FOR statement can be written in terms of other variables. In this case, the highest value is represented by N (the total number of data). Within the loop, each number is read into Value in line 50 and accumulated into Sum in line 60. Once the loop is completed, Sum holds the sum of all the numbers. On execution of line 80, BASIC will write

    SUM OF 5 NUMBERS = 104.3

on the screen.

Use of STEP

In the last example, the STEP modifier was equal to +1. When this is the case, the STEP modifier can be omitted and line 40 can be written as

    40 FOR I=1 TO N

in which case it is assumed that the STEP is equal to +1.

If the step value desired is not equal to +1, the STEP modifier must be included. For example

```
10 REM CONVERT INCHES TO CENTIMETRES
20 PRINT "INCHES", "CENTIMETRES"
30 FOR Inches=5 TO 20 STEP 5
40    Centimetres=2.54*Inches
50    PRINT TAB(0);Inches;TAB(10);Centimetres
60 NEXT Inches:END
```

will convert 5, 10, 15 and 20 inches into centimetres. The output should be as follows:

INCHES	CENTIMETRES
5	12.7
10	25.4
15	38.1
20	50.8

A negative STEP modifier is legal in BASIC. For example

```
10 FOR J=5 TO 1 STEP -1
20    PRINT J
30 NEXT J
40 END
```

will print the values 5, 4, 3, 2 and 1.

For positive step values, the loop is executed so long as the control variable is less than or equal to its final value. For negative step values the loop continues as long as the control variable is greater than or equal to its final value. Note that a FOR-NEXT loop is always executed at least once even if the final value is less than the initial value and a positive STEP is indicated. For example, the loop will be executed once in the following program.

```
10 FOR I=1 TO 0 STEP 1
20    PRINT I
30 NEXT I
40 END
```

Nested FOR-NEXT loops

FOR-NEXT statements can be nested to allow the programming of loops within loops as shown in the example below.

```
10 REM NESTED FOR-NEXT LOOPS
20 FOR K=1 TO 9
30    FOR L=K TO 9
40       PRINT SPC(0);L;
50    NEXT L
60    PRINT
70 NEXT K
80 END
```

On RUNning this program, two loops are set up as follows:

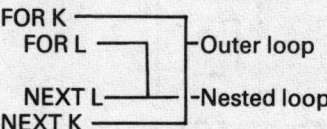

The outer loop is initialized with K=1 and, immediately, the inner, nested loop is executed 9 times. Then the control variable K is incremented by 1, so that now K=2 and the nested loop is executed 8 times. This is repeated until K is equal to 9, when the nested loop is executed only once. The output of this program is as follows:

```
123456789
23456789
3456789
456789
56789
6789
789
89
9
```

The semicolon after the variable L in line 40 allows output to be printed close together on the same line. However, each line of print must be terminated with a line feed (that is, it must send the computer display to the next line). This is provided here by the PRINT statement in line 60. Without it all the numbers now appearing on different lines would be printed on the same line.

---------- Problem 2.3 ----------
Modify the above program so that the output is a square of 15×15 characters, using the letter X as the output character.

Additional levels of nesting are possible. However, deep nesting is costly in terms of memory space. Fig. 2.1 shows some loop configurations, the first five of which are examples of allowable loops, while the sixth is not. Lines joining FOR-NEXT statements must not cross. It is bad programming practice to jump out of FOR-NEXT loops. Programs may work when you do this but the results are unpredictable.

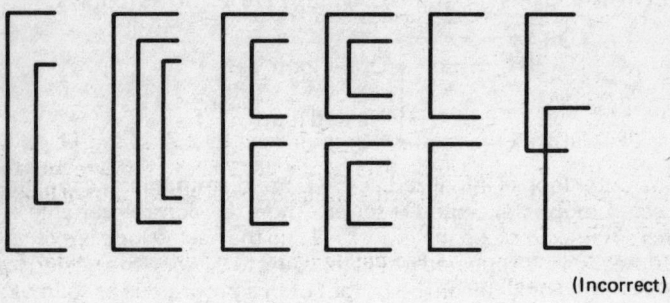

(Incorrect)

Fig. 2.1 Some loop configurations.

Use of FOR-NEXT loops in simple graphics

A limited form of graphics can be achieved with the use of the PRINT statement. For example, consider the following program which will print the letter L in block form.

```
10 PRINT "LL"
20 PRINT "LL"
30 PRINT "LL"
40 PRINT "LL"
50 PRINT "LL"
60 PRINT "LL"
70 PRINT "LL"
80 PRINT "LLLLLLLLL"
90 PRINT "LLLLLLLLL"
100 END
```

Obviously, the use of the PRINT statement in this form is rather cumbersome. However, it is worth noting that the program is made up of only two different types of PRINT statements each repeated several times. The statement of line 10 is repeated seven times, while that of line 80 is repeated twice. It is possible therefore to avoid this repetition by incorporating the FOR-NEXT loop as shown in the program below.

```
10 REM BIG L
20 FOR I=1 TO 9
30    PRINT "LL";
40    IF I>7 THEN PRINT "LLLLLLL":GOTO 60
50    PRINT
60 NEXT I
70 END
```

The FOR-NEXT loop in this program causes the string LL to be printed nine times. When I is equal to 8 and 9, however, the additional string included at the trailer of the IF statement of line 40 is appended to the last two rows.

The above program can be easily adapted to print the letter F in block form, as follows:

```
10 REM BIG F
20 FOR I=1 TO 10
30    PRINT "FF";
40    IF I<3 THEN PRINT "FFFFFFF":GOTO 70
50    IF I=5 OR I=6 THEN PRINT "FFF":GOTO 70
60    PRINT
70 NEXT I
80 END
```

On RUNning the program, BASIC writes

```
FFFFFFFFF
FFFFFFFFF
FF
FF
FFFFF
FFFFF
FF
FF
FF
FF
```

on the screen.

Problem 2.4

Write a similar program to print the letter E in block form. Use two characters for the width of each line of the letter, nine characters for its overall width and ten characters for its height.

It is perhaps worth noting that it is easy to represent letters or other characters in block form provided they are made up of vertical and horizontal lines only. The addition of the PRINT TAB statement is necessary, however, in order to represent a shape such as the letter N which has a diagonal line in it. The program below will print the letter N in block form.

```
10 REM BIG N
20 PRINT "NN";TAB(10);"NN"
30 PRINT "NNN";TAB(10);"NN"
40 FOR I=0 TO 6
50    PRINT "NN";
60    PRINT TAB(I+2);"NN";TAB(10);"NN"
70 NEXT I
80 PRINT "NN";TAB(9);"NNN"
90 PRINT "NN";TAB(10);"NN"
100 END
```

Type this program into your computer, SAVE it and then RUN it. The following shape will appear on your screen.

```
NN            NN
NNN           NN
NNNN          NN
NN NN         NN
NN  NN        NN
NN   NN       NN
NN    NN      NN
NN     NN     NN
NN      NN NN
NN       NNNN
NN        NNN
NN            NN
```

32

Note that lines 20 and 30 provide the first and second row of the block letter, while lines 80 and 90 provide the last two rows. In between, the diagonal stroke of the block letter is printed by line 60 which incorporates a PRINT TAB statement with the loop control variable I as its argument. This has the effect of printing the next row of NN one place to the right each time the FOR-NEXT loop is executed. Now try to incorporate the CLS and TAB(X,Y) statements so that the block letter N prints in the middle of your screen.

WARNING: Jumping out of FOR-NEXT loops can cause your program to fail. If jumping out of such loops is unavoidable, then use the technique given below.

```
10 REM JUMPING OUT OF FOR-NEXT LOOPS
20 INPUT "HOW MANY ENTRIES? " N
30 FOR I=1 TO N
40    INPUT "ENTER A NUMBER " X
50    IF X=999 THEN I=N:GOTO 70
60    PRINT X
70 NEXT I
80 ......
```

Line 50 tests for an input of 999 and if true then I is set to the maximum value of the loop counter so that, when line 70 is reached, the program continues the normal way.

CHAPTER 3
Strings and Arrays

String variables

A sequence of characters is referred to as a literal, and a literal in quotation marks is called a string. For example,

ABC12 is a literal, and "ABC12" is a string.

Like numbers, strings can be assigned to variables. They are distinguished from numeric variables by a $ after the name. For example, A$. The program below assigns a string to the variable named B$ and then PRINTs B$.

```
10 B$="ABC123"
20 PRINT B$
30 END
```

On RUNning the program, BASIC writes

ABC123

on the screen.

The following program will read a string from a DATA statement and assign it to a variable.

```
10 READ AA$
20 PRINT AA$
30 DATA "A1B2"
40 END
```

Several strings can be read and assigned to several variables provided that the strings within the DATA statement are separated by commas. In general, string variables can be used within a BASIC program in the following statements:

(a) A$="ABC" or A$=B$.
(b) READ A$. The string must be in a DATA statement
(c) INPUT A$
(d) PRINT A$
(e) IF A$="YES" THEN ... or IF A$<B$ THEN ... ELSE ...
(f) C$=A$+B$.   This is known as 'concatenation'. It simply joins the second string to the end of the first one.

BASIC assigns a numeric code to each character on the keyboard, according to the ASCII code, as shown in Table 3.1. Thus, each letter of the alphabet is assigned a numeric value and as a result the letter A has a smaller value than B, letter B smaller than C, and so on.

TABLE 3.1 ASCII Conversion Codes

CHAR	ABBR	DEC	CHAR	ABBR	DEC	CHAR	ABBR	DEC
CTRL@	nul	0	CTRL K	vt	11	CTRL V	syn	22
CTRL A	soh	1	CTRL L	ff	12	CTRL W	etb	23
CTRL B	stx	2	CTRL M	cr	13	CTRL X	can	24
CTRL C	etx	3	CTRL N	so	14	CTRL Y	em	25
CTRL D	eot	4	CTRL O	si	15	CTRL Z	sub	26
CTRL E	enq	5	CTRL P	dle	16	CTRL [	esc	27
CTRL F	ack	6	CTRL Q	dc1	17	CTRL \	fs	28
CTRL G	bel	7	CTRL R	dc2	18	CTRL]	gs	29
CTRL H	bs	8	CTRL S	dc3	19	CTRL ^	rs	30
CTRL I	ht	9	CTRL T	dc4	20	CTRL _	us	31
CTRL J	lf	10	CTRL U	nak	21			
SPACE		32	@		64			96
!		33	A		65	a		97
"		34	B		66	b		98
#		35	C		67	c		99
$		36	D		68	d		100
%		37	E		69	e		101
&		38	F		70	f		102
'		39	G		71	g		103
(		40	H		72	h		104
)		41	I		73	i		105
*		42	J		74	j		106
+		43	K		75	k		107
,		44	L		76	l		108
-		45	M		77	m		109
.		46	N		78	n		110
/		47	O		79	o		111
0		48	P		80	p		112
1		49	Q		81	q		113
2		50	R		82	r		114
3		51	S		83	s		115
4		52	T		84	t		116
5		53	U		85	u		117
6		54	V		86	v		118
7		55	W		87	w		119
8		56	X		88	x		120
9		57	Y		89	y		121
:		58	Z		90	z		122
;		59	[		91	{		123
<		60	\		92				124
=		61	]		93	}		125
>		62	^		94	~		126
?		63	_		95	del		127

Note: In the table, groups of two or three lower case letters are abbreviations for standard ASCII control characters. Codes within the range 128 to 255 form the extended IBM character set.

When strings appear in an IF statement as in (e) previously, they are compared character by character from left to right on the basis of the ASCII values until a difference is found. If a character in that position in string A$ has a higher ASCII code than the character in the same position in string B$, then A$ is greater than B$. If all the characters in the same positions are identical but one string has more characters than the other, the longer string is the greater of the two. Thus, alphabetic strings can be placed easily in alphabetical order.

In the statements given so far, the string variables are considered in their entirety. Later on, however, we shall see that with the help of three special string functions, we can access any character within a given string.

String arrays

A number of strings can be stored under a common name in what is known as a string array. Let us assume that we have four names i.e. SMITH, JONES, BROWN and WILSON which we would like to store in a string array. In BASIC, whenever an array is to be used in a program, you must declare your intention to do so in a DIMension statement as shown in the program below, which allows you to read and store the four names into the common variable Name$().

```
10 REM USE OF A STRING ARRAY
20 DIM Name$(4)
30 FOR I=1 TO 4
40    READ Name$(I)
50 NEXT I
60 DATA "SMITH","JONES","BROWN","WILSON"
70 END
```

A simple way to visualize a string array is as follows:

| SMITH | JONES | BROWN | WILSON |

The four names are stored in a common box which has four compartments, each compartment containing one name. Thus, Name$(2) refers to the 2nd compartment of string array Name$(), and Name$(4) to the 4th compartment. The DIM statement tells BASIC that a string array called Name$() is to be used with maximum dimensions as given within the brackets following the array name (in this case 4). Finally, any reference to an array name within a program must be of the form

Name$(I)

where I has a value between 0 and the maximum number given in the DIM statement. Note that the statement DIM Name$(4) reserves, in fact, five compartments starting with the Name$(0) compartment. Reference to Name$ alone does not refer to the array, but to the unsubscripted string variable Name$, which merely happens to be using the same letters.

The following program will READ from a DATA statement the name, location and telephone extension of five employees. Note that the data have been structured so that the commas separating the names from the locations and the locations from the telephone extensions have the same position within each string. This is achieved by adding spaces to compensate for different lengths of names etc. We do this at this stage in order to allow manipulation of these strings later. In the example, two FOR-NEXT loops are used to demonstrate that once data have been READ, they are stored in memory (unless overwritten). One loop would normally be sufficient.

```
10 REM EMPLOYEES
20 DIM Employee$(5)
30 FOR I=1 TO 5:READ Employee$(I):NEXT I
40 FOR I=1 TO 5:PRINT Employee$(I):NEXT I
310 DATA "WILSON M. ,ROOM 1.24,  395"
320 DATA "SMITH M.   ,ROOM 2.6 ,7315"
330 DATA "JONES B.M.,ROOM 6.19,1698"
340 DATA "SMITH A.A. ,ROOM 2.12,  456"
350 DATA "BROWN C.   ,ROOM 3.1 ,  432"
400 END
```

Type this program using the same line numbers as those given above, SAVE it under the filename EMPLOY and RUN it. BASIC will write the literals on the screen as they appear within the DATA statements, but without the quotation marks, as follows:

```
WILSON M. ,ROOM 1.24,  395
SMITH M.   ,ROOM 2.6 ,7315
JONES B.M.,ROOM 6.19,1698
SMITH A.A. ,ROOM 2.12,  456
BROWN C.   ,ROOM 3.1 ,  432
```

String functions

We shall now introduce some functions which allow string manipulation. For example, suppose we want to extract and print out only the names of the employees held in array Employee$(). BASIC allows us to do this quite easily with the function

LEFT$()

The few program lines following, when added to the previous program will achieve this.

```
140 PRINT
150 FOR I=1 TO 5
160    PRINT LEFT$(Employee$(I),10)
170 NEXT I
```

Note that the function LEFT$ has two bracketed arguments; first is the Ith string of string array Employee$() and second is the numeral 10 which refers to the number of characters of interest. The function, together with the PRINT statement, causes the 10 leftmost characters of Employee$(I) to be printed. Type these additional lines and try the program.

Another string function allows manipulation of the rightmost characters of a string. This is achieved by the use of the function

    RIGHT$()

To illustrate its use, change line 160 of the program to

    160 PRINT LEFT$(Employee$(I),10),RIGHT$(Employee$(I),4)

and RUN it. You will see that the second column of the last PRINT statement contains the four rightmost characters of each string.

A third function which allows information to be extracted from the middle of a string is

    MID$()

Substituting line 160 in the program with the line given below, will print the location of each employee.

    160 PRINT MID$(Employee$(I),12,9)

Note that this function requires two numeric values to follow the Ith string. The first is the starting point within a string (12th character here) and the second is the number of characters to be considered (9 in this case). However, if the second number were to be omitted from the argument list, then the characters considered would start at the first number and finish at the end of the string.

As an example of the use of string arrays, consider the program following, which causes information on the quantity and price of several items in stock to be stored by BASIC. To extract information regarding details of items in stock, simply start the program and answer the questions posed.

Firstly, the program reads and stores into string array Item$() the actual names of the items in stock, while at the same time their quantity and price are read into Stock$(). In response to the question 'WHICH ITEM', the name of an item, associated with the string variable Name$, is typed in. If it is END, then the program stops. If, however, it has any other name, it causes a loop to be set up (lines 70 to 110) which compares in turn the contents of Item$() with Name$. If they are found to be equal, it prints the required information held in Stock$(), otherwise it executes line 120.

```
10 REM STOCKTAKING
20 DIM Item$(4),Stock$(4)
30 FOR I=1 TO 4:READ Item$(I),Stock$(I):NEXT I
40 REPEAT:PRINT
50    INPUT "WHICH ITEM? " Name$
60    IF Name$="END" THEN END
70    FOR I=1 TO 4
80       IF Item$(I)<>Name$ GOTO 100
90       PRINT ">>>>>>> ";LEFT$(Stock$(I),3);
            " IN STOCK AT $"; RIGHT$(Stock$(I),4);" EACH"
100   NEXT I
110 UNTIL FALSE
120 DATA "INK ERASER","200,0.10"
130 DATA "PENCIL ERASER","320,0.15"
140 DATA "TYPING ERASER","25 ,0.25"
150 DATA "CORRECTION FLUID","150,0.50"
```

Type this program carefully, paying particular attention to the spaces inserted within the various PRINT and DATA statements. SAVE it under file name STOCK.

On RUNning the program, BASIC responds with

WHICH ITEM?

and awaits your response. Below, we present a typical RUN of this program.

WHICH ITEM? PENCIL

WHICH ITEM? PENCIL ERASER

>>>>>> 320 IN STOCK AT $0.15 EACH

WHICH ITEM? CORRECTION FLUID

>>>>>> 150 IN STOCK AT $0.5 EACH

WHICH ITEM? END

which causes the program to end.

―――――――――――――――――― **Problem 3.1** ――――――――――――――

(a) Modify the above stocktaking program so that you only need to enter the first three letters of each item whenever the question 'WHICH ITEM' is asked. The output of your program should, however, print the full name of each item.

(b) Having carried out modification (a), now restructure the data so that each data line is read into one member of a string array. Use the LEFT$(), RIGHT$() and MID$() functions to extract the appropriate information for the printout.

―――――――――――――――――――――――――――――――――――

The need for structuring the data (e.g. with spaces) can lead to mistakes when typing information into a DATA line, especially in the case of numerical data. In fact, numerical data can be stored in a numerical array without the need for structuring them within the DATA statement. This leads to a much greater programming flexibility, and will be investigated in the following section.

Subscripted numeric variables

Subscripted variables permit the representation of many quantities with one variable name. A particular quantity is indicated by writing a subscript in parentheses after the variable name. Individual quantities are called elements, while a set of elements is called an array. A subscripted variable may have one, two or three subscripts, and it then represents a one- two- or three-dimensional array.

The elements of a one-dimensional array can be represented as follows:

     A(0)   A(1)   A(2)   A(3)   A(4)

while those of a two-dimensional array as:

    A(0,0)   A(0,1)   A(0,2)   A(0,3)
    A(1,0)   A(1,1)   A(1,2)   A(1,3)
    A(2,0)   A(2,1)   A(2,2)   A(2,3)

The first of the two subscripts refers to the row number, running from 0 to the maximum number of declared rows, and the second subscript to the column number, running from 0 to the maximum number of declared columns.

A three-dimensional array can be thought of as stacked two-dimensional arrays with the third subscript, running from 0 to the maximum height of the stack.

In the computer, however, arrays are stored with elements following one another on a single line as shown below.

   A(0,0)   A(1,0)   A(2,0)   A(0,1)   A(1,1)   A(2,1)

with the first subscript changing more rapidly than the second, and the second more rapidly than the third (in the case of a three-dimensional array). Provided that this is recognized and understood, we can use the previous pictorial form of representation for programming purposes.

Numerical arrays must be declared prior to their use in a DIM statement just as we had to declare string arrays. The form of the statement is shown below.

   DIM X(15), Y(3,5), Z(3,5,4)

where array X() has been declared to be a one-dimensional array with a maximum of 16 elements (don't forget the zero'th element), array Y(,) has been declared as a two-dimensional array of 4 rows and 6 columns, and array Z(,,) as a three-dimensional array of 4 rows and 6 columns stacked 5 deep.

The following program illustrates the use of numerical arrays. Data are read into a one-dimensional array and subsequently the contents of the even numbered elements are summed into variable Even, while the contents of all the odd elements are summed into variable Odd.

```
10 REM NUMERICAL ARRAY
20 DIM Number(15)
30 REM READ & STORE INTO Number() 16 NUMBERS
40 FOR I=0 TO 15:READ Number(I):NEXT I
50 REM SUM EVEN ELEMENTS
60 Even=0
70 FOR I=0 TO 14 STEP 2:Even=Even+Number(I):NEXT I
80 REM SUM ODD ELEMENTS
90 Odd=0
100 FOR I=1 TO 15 STEP 2:Odd=Odd+Number(I):NEXT I
110 REM PRINT CONTENTS OF ARRAY
120 FOR I=0 TO 15:PRINT Number(I):NEXT I:PRINT
130 PRINT "EVEN=";Even,"ODD=";Odd
140 DATA 4,7,6,1,9,7,14,39,24,19,32,21,8,5,15,28
150 END
```

On RUNning this program, the contents of array Number(), which are the numbers listed in line 140, are PRINTed out one under the other. Under these the output

   EVEN=112 ODD=127

appears on the screen.

There are four error messages which relate to the use of arrays. These are:

> Array
> Bad DIM
> DIM space
> Subscript

The first is caused if an array is not dimensioned, the second if an array has been dimensioned with a negative number of elements, the third if an attempt is made to use an array for which there is insufficient room in the computer's memory and the fourth if an attempt has been made to use an array element that is outside the declared dimension.

Note. Had we used the previous program to store more than 20 numbers and then attempted to print them on the screen in a vertical format, we would lose the beginning of the printout as the screen scrolled upwards. To halt program execution temporarily, press

> 'CTRL'SHIFT

To restart program execution from the point of interruption, release the SHIFT key. Try this command by modifying the previous program so that it READs, stores and PRINTs 30 numbers.

We shall now modify the original stocktaking program so that the numerical parts of the data are stored in a two-dimensional array. After you have studied it, carry out a similar modification to your version of the stocktaking program resulting from part (a) of Problem 3.1.

```
10 REM STOCKTAKING USING STRINGS & ARRAYS
20 DIM Item$(4),Stock(4,2)
30 FOR I=1 TO 4:READ Item$(I),Stock(I,1),Stock(I,2):
   NEXT I
40 REPEAT:PRINT
50    INPUT "WHICH ITEM? " Name$
60    IF Name$="END" THEN END
70    FOR I=1 TO 4
80       IF Item$(I)<>Name$ GOTO 100
90       PRINT ">>>>> ";Stock(I,1);" IN STOCK AT$";
         Stock(I,2);" EACH"
100   NEXT I
110 UNTIL FALSE
120 DATA "INK ERASER",200,0.1
130 DATA "PENCIL ERASER",320,0.15
140 DATA "TYPING ERASER",25,0.25
150 DATA "CORRECTION FLUID",150,0.5
```

Note how much easier it is to structure the DATA statements when using numeric arrays rather than string arrays for numeric data.

Problem 3.2

The first two numbers of the number series given below are 1 and 1. The next number in the sequence is the sum of these two and subsequent numbers are the sum of the preceding pair. So we get:

$$1, 1, 2, 3, 5, 8, 13, 21, ...$$

Write a program to calculate the first N numbers of the series (where N is an input to the program) and store them in an appropriate one-dimensional numeric array. In a second one-dimensional array, store the average of adjacent pairs of numbers. Print the output in two columns under appropriate headings.

Some more string functions
In this section we shall introduce the following additional string functions.

ASC( ), CHR$( ), LEN( ), STR$( ), EVAL() and VAL( )

Examples of the use of these functions are given below.

ASCII conversion
    N=ASC("ABCD")

will return the decimal ASCII code for the first character of the string enclosed in the brackets of the function. In this case, 65 will be returned (see Table 3.1).

Character conversion
    C$=CHR$(66)

will return the ASCII character that corresponds to the value of the argument, in this case the letter B. The value of the argument must lie between 0 and 255.

Length of string
    L=LEN("XYZ")

will return the value of length of the string, that is, the number of characters in the string. In this case L will be set to 3.

String conversion
    S$=STR$(X)

where X is a numeric variable which might be the result of a calculation. Using the function STR$() will convert the value of the argument into a string. In this case, if X had the value of 98.56, say, then S$ becomes equal to "98.56".

Evaluate a string

  X=EVAL(A$)

where A$ is a string containing a mathematical expression such as

  A$="2*Y+C"

Provided the values of both Y and C are known prior to attempting to use this function, it will evaluate the mathematical expression in A$ and pass its value to X.

Value of string
If R$ represents a string given by

  R$="3.123E12 METRES"

then the statement

  X=VAL(R$)

will return the value of the string up to the first non-numeric character, in this case 3.123E+12. If the string begins with a non-numeric character then the value 0 is returned.

String concatenation
BASIC allows the concatenation (joining together) of strings. We shall illustrate this facility by considering the following program in which the computer asks you to enter your surname first followed by your first name. It then concatenates the two (first name first followed by surname with a space in between) and prints the result which is held in string variable X$.

```
10 REM CONCATENATION
20 CLS:INPUT "ENTER YOUR SURNAME PLEASE " S$:
   PRINT
30 INPUT "ENTER YOUR FIRST NAME PLEASE " N$
40 X$=N$ + " " + S$
50 CLS:PRINT "HELLO ";X$
60 END
```

As it stands, the program is rather trivial. However, using concatenation together with some of the string functions mentioned earlier, can result in a somewhat more spectacular result. To illustrate this, add the following lines to the program given above.

```
50 CLS:L=LEN(X$):IF L>22 THEN X$=LEFT$(N$,1)
   + ". " + S$: L=LEN(X$)
60 FOR I=1 TO L:PRINT MID$(X$,I,1);:IF I=1 THEN
   PRINT " ";X$;
70 IF I=L THEN PRINT " ";X$;
80 PRINT TAB(L+4);MID$(X$,I,1):NEXT I
90 END
```

RUN the program and supply it with your full name (surname first). What you will see on the screen, if your name was JOHN BROWN, would be:

```
J  JOHN BROWN  J
O              O
H              H
N              N
B              B
R              R
O              O
W              W
N  JOHN BROWN  N
```

Note that the program has worked out the length of your full name and allowed enough space between the two vertical columns to write it horizontally on the first and last rows. Now re-RUN the program, but this time type in a really long name, say CHRISTOPHER VERYLONGFELLOW. Can you work out from the program lines and the output on your screen what has happened? Try it. You can always remove the third and fourth statements of line 50 to see what the effect would be without their presence when dealing with very long names.

Perhaps the most important use of concatenation is that of building up strings by overlaying. What we mean by this is the ability to create an empty string of a fixed length and then place characters in it anywhere along its length, in any order we choose. The following program will help to illustrate this effect.

```
10 REM OVERLAYING
20 L$=" "
30 FOR I=1 TO 39:L$=L$+" ":NEXT I
40 A$="*"
50 INPUT "HOW MANY STARS? " N
60 FOR I=1 TO N
70    PRINT "POSITION ";I;:INPUT "? " P:IF P<2 OR P>38
      THEN PRINT "RE-ENTER":GOTO 70
80    L$=LEFT$(L$,P-1) + A$ + MID$(L$,P+1)
90 NEXT I
100 PRINT:
    PRINT "123456789012345678901234567890123456789"
110 PRINT L$:END
```

Lines 20 and 30 create an empty string, L$, 40 characters long. Subsequently, we overlay a number of asterisks (string A$) onto the empty string L$. This is achieved by specifying the position P in which we wish to place an asterisk and concatenating the leftmost P-1 characters already in string L$ to string A$ and then concatenate to the resultant string the remaining characters within string L$ from position P+1 to the end of the string. The result is then stored in L$. The process can be repeated as many times as we choose. Note that unlike the PRINT TAB procedure, with this method we can 'tabulate' backwards.

On RUNning the program, BASIC will respond with a series of questions. Enter the numbers following the question marks.

```
HOW MANY STARS? 3
POSITION 1? 35
POSITION 2? 24
POSITION 3? 12

12345678901234567890123456789012345678 90
           *           *            *
```

The numbers above the asterisks are only printed so that we can check the exact position of each asterisk.

This overlaying technique will be used later on when we come to consider right-justification and formatting of numbers.

Problem 3.3

Write a program which uses one or more string functions to allow:

(a) the printing of a given letter specified by entering a number within the range from 1 to 26, and

(b) the printing of a number corresponding to the position of a given letter within the alphabet, by entering any given letter.

Alphabetical sorting

Many programming applications, such as manipulation of information on employees' records, require alphabetical sorting. To achieve this, we must draw on the technique developed earlier on for sorting numbers, as well as program 'Three number sort'.

The technique we shall adopt is more or less the same as the one used previously except that string arrays are used rather than individual variables. This has the effect of reducing the required number of IF statements to one. The technique is illustrated as follows by applying it to the 'Employees' program which should have been stored under the filename EMPLOY. Additions to the program are incorporated between lines 20 and 300. LOAD the EMPLOY program and make these changes. Your program should now look as follows:

```
10 REM ALPHABETICAL SORTING
20 READ N:DIM Employee$(N)
30 FOR I=1 TO N:READ Employee$(I):NEXT I
40 FOR I=1 TO N:PRINT Employee$(I):NEXT I
50 PRINT:PRINT:PRINT "SORTED INFORMATION"
110 FOR I=1 TO N-1
120    IF Employee$(I)>Employee$(I+1) THEN
       Temporary$=Employee$(I+1):
       Employee$(I+1)=Employee$(I):
       Employee$(I)=Temporary$
130 NEXT I
150 FOR I=1 TO N:PRINT Employee$(I):NEXT I
300 DATA 5
310 DATA "WILSON M.  ,ROOM 1.24, 395"
320 DATA "SMITH M.   ,ROOM 2.6 ,7315"
330 DATA "JONES B.M. ,ROOM 6.19,1698"
340 DATA "SMITH A.A. ,ROOM 2.12, 456"
350 DATA "BROWN C.   ,ROOM 3.1 , 432"
400 END
```

Make sure that the line numbers of your program correspond to those shown above, as additional lines will shortly be added.

On RUNning the above program you will see that the first five lines print the employees in the same order as they appear in the DATA statements. The second five lines are the result of executing the FOR-NEXT loop of statements 110 to 130. Within this loop, when I=1 the first string is compared with the second and if it is found to be smaller, control is passed to line 130 otherwise the two strings are interchanged (at the trailer of the IF statement of line 120). When I=2 the second string is compared with the third, and so on until I=N-1, when the (N-1)th string is compared with the Nth. The result in our case is that BROWN has moved one position up as follows:

```
WILSON  M.,ROOM 1.24, 395
SMITH   M.,ROOM 2.6 ,7315
JONES   B.M.,ROOM 6.19,1698
SMITH   A.A.,ROOM 2.12, 456
BROWN   C.,ROOM 3.1 , 432

SORTED INFORMATION
SMITH   M.,ROOM 2.6 ,7315
JONES   B.M.,ROOM 6.19,1698
SMITH   A.A.,ROOM 2.12, 456
BROWN   C.,ROOM 3.1 , 432
WILSON  M.,ROOM 1.24, 395
```

In order for BROWN to move to the top of the list we must repeat the FOR-NEXT loop of lines 110 to 130, N-1 times. We shall do this by adding an extra FOR-NEXT loop as follows:

```
100 FOR J=1 TO N-1
180 NEXT J
```

Type these two lines into the computer and RUN the program. You will see that although all the information appears on the screen it is rather difficult to distinguish the result of each execution of the outer FOR-NEXT loop. The addition of the following two lines should put this right.

```
140 PRINT:PRINT:PRINT TAB(0);J
160 Key$=GET$
```

The GET$ statement forces the computer to fetch information from the keyboard and, in this case, assign it to Key$. The computer will wait until you press a key before it can carry on with the rest of the program. This means that the results of each iteration of the J loop can be studied at leisure before continuing with program execution (by pressing any key except ESCAPE). Add these lines and re-RUN the program. What you will see on the screen is:

SORTED INFORMATION

1
SMITH   M.,ROOM 2.6 ,7315
JONES B.M.,ROOM 6.19,1698
SMITH A.A.,ROOM 2.12, 456
BROWN   C.,ROOM 3.1 , 432
WILSON   M.,ROOM 1.24, 395

2
JONES B.M.,ROOM 6.19,1698
SMITH A.A.,ROOM 2.12, 456
BROWN   C.,ROOM 3.1 , 432
SMITH   M.,ROOM 2.6 ,7315
WILSON   M.,ROOM 1.24, 395

3
JONES B.M.,ROOM 6.19,1698
BROWN   C.,ROOM 3.1 , 432
SMITH A.A.,ROOM 2.12, 456
SMITH   M.,ROOM 2.6 ,7315
WILSON   M.,ROOM 1.24, 395

4
BROWN   C.,ROOM 3.1 , 432
JONES B.M.,ROOM 6.19,1698
SMITH A.A.,ROOM 2.12, 456
SMITH   M.,ROOM 2.6 ,7315
WILSON   M.,ROOM 1.24, 395

The bubble sort technique

From the output of the above program you will notice two things:

(a) After the first execution of the J loop, WILSON drops to the end of the list, and after every subsequent iteration the next highest valued name appears above WILSON.

(b) After each iteration of the J loop, BROWN moves up one position in the list of names.

This means that there is room for improving the program in two ways. Since the highest valued name drops to the bottom of the list, we can reduce the upper limit of the I loop by one for each execution of the J loop. Also, while the full N-1 iterations may be needed in the worst case, the list will often be sorted in somewhere between 0 and N-1 iterations. This can be overcome by incorporating a 'flag' in the program whose value is set to 0 normally, but is reset to 1 every time an exchange takes place. By testing for the value of the flag at the end of each iteration we can tell whether or not we need to execute the J loop once more.

The addition of lines 90, 105, 170 and second statement in line 120, as well as the change of the variable representing the upper limit of the control variable I in line 110, cover both suggestions for improving the program's efficiency. The resulting program is listed below. SAVE this program under the filename BUBBLE.

```
10 REM BUBBLE SORT
20 READ N: DIM Employee$(N)
30 FOR I=1 TO N: READ Employee$(I): NEXT I
40 FOR I=1 TO N: PRINT Employee$(I): NEXT I
50 PRINT: PRINT: PRINT "SORTED INFORMATION"
90 M=N
100 FOR J=1 TO N-1
105    M=M-1:Flag=0
110    FOR I=1 TO M
120       IF Employee$(I)>Employee$(I+1) THEN Flag=1:
          Temporary$=Employee$(I+1):Employee$(I+1)
          =Employee$(I) :Employee$(I)=Temporary$
130    NEXT I
140    PRINT: PRINT: PRINT TAB(0);J
150    FOR I=1 TO N: PRINT Employee$(I): NEXT I
160    Key$=GET$
170    IF Flag=0 GOTO 400
180 NEXT J
300 DATA 5
310 DATA "WILSON M.,ROOM 1.24,  395"
320 DATA "SMITH M.,ROOM 2.6 ,7315"
330 DATA "JONES B.M.,ROOM 6.19,1698"
340 DATA "SMITH A.A.,ROOM 2.12, 456"
350 DATA "BROWN C.,ROOM 3.1 , 432"
400 END
```

Variable M is used in line 90 as a temporary store for the total number of strings to be manipulated each time the J loop is executed. Its value is first made equal to N and subsequently it is reduced by one in line 105, thus reducing the value of the upper limit of the control variable I in line 110. This reduces the total number of string comparisons to a minimum. The constant Flag in lines 105 and 170 is used as an indicator. Its value is set to 1 to indicate that a string interchange has taken place. If Flag remains 0 for the whole of the I loop, then it indicates that the strings are in the required order.

Sending output to a printer

We have already seen in the Introduction that information can be sent to a a printer by typing the command

    'CTRL'B

which causes all subsequent information typed on the keyboard and LISTed or PRINTed from within the program to be transferred to the printer. The command

    'CTRL'C

disconnects the printer.

Commands can also be used from within a BASIC program with the CHR$() function as shown below. To connect the printer from within a BASIC program, include the statement

    VDU 2   or   PRINT CHR$(2)

at the appropriate place. To disconnect the printer, use the statement

    VDU 3   or   PRINT CHR$(3)

This must appear in a program after the statement which caused output to be printed.

The following program will PRINT the string XYZ on the printer.

```
10 REM PRINT OUTPUT ON PRINTER
20 S$="XYZ"
30 REPEAT:INPUT "OUTPUT TO SCREEN OR PRINTER?
   (S/P) " Q$
40 UNTIL Q$="S" OR Q$="P"
50 IF LEFT$(Q$,1)="P" THEN VDU2
60 PRINT S$
70 VDU3
80 END
```

―――――――――――――――――― **Problem 3.4** ――――――――――――――
Incorporate the above facility for printing the output of the BUBBLE program either on the screen or on the printer. All additional lines to achieve this should be added between existing lines 30 and 40. Disconnection from the printer should be inserted in line 400.

CHAPTER 4

Subprograms

Standard arithmetic functions

BASIC contains functions to perform many mathematical operations. They relieve the user from programming his own small routines to calculate such common functions as logarithms, square roots, sines of angles, and so on. BASIC's mathematical functions have a three-letter call name followed by a parenthesized argument. They are pre-defined and may be used anywhere in a program. Some of BASIC's most common standard functions are listed below.

TABLE 4.1 Standard BASIC Functions

Call Name	Function
SIN(X)	Sine of angle X, where X is in radians
COS(X)	Cosine of angle X, where X is in radians
TAN(X)	Tangent of angle X, where X is in radians
ASN(X) ACS(X) ATN(X)	Arc-sine of X Arc-cosine of X Arc-tangent of X. These return the angle in radians in the range +1.570796 to −1.570796
DEG(X)	Converts X radians to degrees
RAD(X)	Converts X degrees to radians
SQR(X)	Returns the square root of X
EXP(X)	Raises e to the power of X
LOG(X)	Returns the logarithm to base 10 of X
LN(X)	Returns the natural logarithm of X
ABS(X)	Returns the absolute value of X
SGN(X)	Returns 1, 0 or −1 to indicate the sign of X
INT(X)	Returns the truncated integer part of X
RND(X)	Generates a random number which depends on the value of X

Function calls can be used as expressions or elements of expressions wherever expressions are legal. The argument X of the function can be a constant, a variable, an expression or another function. A further explanation of the use of these functions is given below.

SIN(X), COS(X) and TAN(X)
The sine, cosine and tangent functions require an argument angle expressed in radians. If the angle is stated in degrees, conversion to radians can be achieved with the function RAD().

ASN(X), ACS(X) and ATN(X)
The arc-sine, arc-cosine and arc-tangent functions return a value in radians, in the range +1.570796 to −1.570796 corresponding to the value of a sine, cosine or tangent supplied as the argument X. Conversion to degrees is achieved with the function DEG().

SQR(X)
The SQR() function returns the square root of the number supplied to it.

We shall illustrate the use of the above functions by considering a simple problem involving a 2 m long ladder resting against a wall. We assume that the angle between ladder and ground is 60 degrees and with the help of simple trigonometry we shall work out the vertical distance between the top of the ladder and the ground, the horizontal distance between the foot of the ladder and the wall and also the ratio of the vertical to horizontal distance.

The program uses the trigonometric functions SIN(), COS(), TAN(), ATAN() and also the functions DEG(), RAD() and SQR() to solve the problem. In addition, it calculates the original angle and ladder length.

```
10 REM LADDER AGAINST WALL
20 Angle=60:REM IN DEGREES
30 Arads=RAD(Angle):REM IN RADS
40 Vert=2*SIN(Arads)
50 Horiz=2*COS(Arads)
60 Ratio=TAN(Arads)
70 PRINT "ORIG ANGLE=";Angle
80 PRINT "VERT DIST=";Vert
90 PRINT "HORIZ DIST=";Horiz
100 PRINT "RATIO=";Ratio
110 Arads2=ATN(Vert/Horiz)
120 Angle2=DEG(Arads2)
130 PRINT "CALC ANGLE=";Angle2
140 Length=SQR(Vert^2 + Horiz^2)
150 PRINT "CALC LADDER LENGTH=";Length
160 END
```

On RUNning the program, BASIC will respond with

```
ORIG ANGLE=60
VERT DIST=1.73205081
HORIZ DIST=1
RATIO=1.73205081
CALC ANGLE=60
CALC LADDER LENGTH=2
```

EXP(X)

The exponential function raises the number e to the power of X. The EXP() function is the inverse of the LN() function. The relationship is

$$LN(EXP(X)) = X$$

LOG(X) and LN(X)

The logarithms to base 10 and base e are given by these functions. Antilogarithm functions are not given but they can easily be derived using the following identities:

Antilog(X)=10^X (base 10)   =e^X (base e. This is EXP(X))

ABS(X)

The ABS() function returns the absolute (that is, positive) value of a given number. For example ABS(1.234) is 1.234, while ABS(−2.345) is returned as 2.345.

SGN(X)

The sign function returns 1 if X is positive, 0 if X=0, and −1 if X is negative.

INT(X)

The integer function returns the value of X rounded down to the nearest integer. Thus, INT(6.97) returns the value 6, whilst INT(−6.789) returns the value −7.

Numbers can be rounded to the nearest whole number, rather than rounding down, by using the function INT(X+0.5). For example, INT(5.67+0.5) returns the value 6. It can also be used to round to (a) any given number of decimal places or (b) to the nearest integer power of 10, by the following expression:

INT(X*10^D+0.5)/10^D

where D is (a) a positive integer or (b) a negative integer supplied by the user. For rounding to the first decimal, D=1; to the nearest 100, D=-2. The program following will help to illustrate these points.

```
10 REM ROUNDING NUMBERS
20 REPEAT
30    INPUT "ENTER A NUMBER " X
40    INPUT "HOW MANY DEC PLACES? " D
50    N=INT(X*10^D+0.5)/10^D
60    PRINT N:PRINT
70 UNTIL FALSE
```

Type the program and RUN it. Results of a typical RUN are given below.

```
ENTER A NUMBER 1.23456
HOW MANY DEC PLACES? 3
   1.235

ENTER A NUMBER 25.6789
HOW MANY DEC PLACES? 2
   25.68

ENTER A NUMBER 120.5
HOW MANY DEC PLACES? -2
   100
```

Try it yourself. To stop the program press the ESCAPE key.

RND(X)

This function is used to produce random numbers. The numbers are not truly random as they can be reproduced at will. However, they will pass all the randomness tests. Random number generators start from a 'seed number' and produce a series of numbers based on the seed. By using the same seed again, the same series of numbers can be obtained. Random numbers are used in statistical programs and in all kinds of simulations from simple games to complex computer models. The value returned by the RND() function depends on the argument, that is the number in brackets following RND.

RND	by itself produces a whole random number between -2147483648 and 2147483647. These limits have been taken from the BBC-BASIC86 Manual; we have not tested them all!
RND(-X)	resets the seed to a value based on X and returns the value X.
RND(0)	repeats the last number generated by RND(1). It only works if the RND() function has not been used since the last use of RND(1).
RND(1)	produces a random number between 0 and .99999999.
RND(X)	generates an integer value between and including 1 and X.

In some programs, especially business simulations, it is necessary to reproduce the same 'random' conditions from RUN to RUN. This is done with the dice throwing program given below. Type the program and RUN it. You should produce the same 'random' throws as shown below. Note that both sets of throws produce the same numbers because of the statement in line 40.

```
10 REM THROWING DICE
20 FOR J=1 TO 2
30   PRINT TAB(7);"THROW        NUMBER"
40   X=RND(-3)
50   FOR I=1 TO 6:PRINT I,RND(6):NEXT I
60 NEXT J:END
```

On RUNning the program the following output is printed on the screen.

THROW	NUMBER
1	1
2	6
3	3
4	2
5	4
6	4
THROW	NUMBER
1	1
2	6
3	3
4	2
5	4
6	4

In some contexts it is a severe disadvantage to have the same series of random numbers produced. This will often happen, however, when the machine is first switched on. Because the random number seed is reset to the same value after switching on, the same series will be produced. You could deal the same set of cards each time you switched on and used a poker playing game! To overcome this problem, you must set the seed to a random value. Type

X=RND(-TIME)

before loading programs using random numbers and the problem is solved. The random number seed is now set to the value of the internal clock which will have a different value whenever it is used. Change line 40 of the previous program to

40 X=RND(-TIME)

and re-RUN it. Each time the program is RUN a different series of values will be produced.

Derived mathematical functions

Some useful mathematical functions which can be derived from standard BASIC functions are listed below.

TABLE 4.2 Derived Mathematical Functions

Function	Formula

TRIGONOMETRIC

Cosecant	CSC(X)=1/SIN(X)
Cotangent	COT(X)=1/TAN(X)
Secant	SEC(X)=1/COS(X)

INVERSE TRIGONOMETRIC

Arc Cosecant	ACSC(X)=ATN(1/SQR(X*X−1))+(SGN(X)-1)*PI/2
Arc Cotangent	ACOT(X)=-ATN(X)+PI/2
Arc Secant	ASEC(X)=ATN(SQR(X*X−1))+(SGN(X)−1)*PI/2

HYPERBOLIC

Hyp Cosine	COSH(X)=(EXP(X)+EXP(−X))/2
Hyp Sine	SINH(X)=(EXP(X)-EXP(−X))/2
Hyp Tangent	TANH(X)=-EXP(−X)/(EXP(X)+EXP(−X))*2+1
Hyp Cosecant	CSCH(X)=2/(EXP(X)-EXP(−X))
Hyp Cotangent	COTH(X)=EXP(−X)/(EXP(X)-EXP(−X))*2+1
Hyp Secant	SECH(X)=2/(EXP(X)+EXP(−X))

INVERSE HYPERBOLIC

Arc Cosh	ACOSH(X)=LOG(X+SQR(X*X−1))
Arc Sinh	ASINH(X)=LOG(X+SQR(X*X+1))
Arc Tanh	ATANH(X)=LOG((1+X)/(1−X))/2
Arc Cosech	ACSCH(X)=LOG((SGN(X)*SQR(X*X+1)+1)/X)
Arc Cotanh	ACOTH(X)=LOG((X+1)/(X−1))/2
Arc Sech	ASECH(X)=LOG((SQR(−X*X+1)+1)/X)

Note. *The constant PI used in the formulae above is a standard BBC-BASIC constant and has the value of 3.141592654.*

User-defined functions

In some programs it may be necessary to use the same mathematical expression in several places, often using different data. BASIC user-defined functions enable definition of unique operations or expressions. These can then be called in the same manner as standard functions.

The user-defined function is identified by a special call name followed by a parenthesized argument. The first two letters of the function name must be FN, while the rest of the letters may be any legitimate variable name. Such a function however, must be defined using the DEF statement which, in general, is placed at the beginning of a program. Multi-line DEFinitions must be placed at the end of the main program, that is, after the END statement. The following program illustrates the use of a single-line user-defined function.

```
10 REM SINGLE-LINE USER-DEFINED FUNCTION
20 REM AREA OF A CIRCLE
30 DEF FNArea(R)=PI*R^2
40 FOR I=1 TO 10
50    A=FNArea(I)
60    PRINT TAB(0);I,A
70 NEXT I
80 END
```

The program calculates the areas of circles with radii of integer values between 1 and 10. The formula is given in the DEF FNArea() statement of line 30. The constant PI used in the formula is a standard BBC-BASIC constant and has the value of 3.141592654. The value for the radius is passed to the function via a parenthesized variable known as the function parameter or argument. Note that the variable name representing this parameter need not be the same as that used in the calling statement within the main body of the program. When called, the parenthesized argument may be any legal expression; its value is simply substituted for the function variable.

The program below which calculates the volume of a cylinder, is used to illustrate multi-line user-defined functions. SAVE this under the filename VOLUME.

```
10 REM MULTI-LINE USER-DEFINED FUNCTION
20 REM VOLUME OF A CYLINDER
30 INPUT "RADIUS OF CYLINDER? " Radius
40 INPUT "HEIGHT OF CYLINDER? " Height
50 PRINT "VOLUME=";FNVolume(Radius,Height)
60 END
10000 DEF FNVolume(R,H)
10010 Basearea=PI*R^2
10020 V=Basearea*H
10030 =V
```

The function is defined in lines 10000 to 10030 and two parameters are passed to it. Radius and Height are the actual parameters and the numbers held in them are passed to the two formal parameters R and H. Note the form of the last line of the DEFinition; it says that FNVolume has the value of V.

In this example, we have spread the function DEFinition on several lines in order to illustrate the format of multi-line DEFinitions. We could quite easily re-write the whole function on one line as

```
10000 DEF FNVolume(R,H)=PI*R^2*H
```

Further, we have calculated the Basearea of the cylinder separately in order to demonstrate local and global variables.

The symbols parenthesized in the DEF line are called formal parameters. All formal parameters (such as R and H in line 10000) are local variables which means that their value is only known to the function. All other variables are called global variables which means that their values are known to both the function and the main program. In order to illustrate this last point, add the following line to the above program (using the four line DEFinition given above):

    55 PRINT TAB(0);Basearea;TAB(15);V

and re-RUN it. You will see that the values held in Basearea and V are accessible from the main program even though these values were calculated in the function after the call to it from the main program.

We can declare a variable or a number of variables within a function to be local with the use of the statement

    LOCAL X,Y,Z

In the above example, if we wanted both Basearea and V to be LOCAL to the function, we would have to add the following line:

    10005 LOCAL Basearea,V

To illustrate that this is the case add the following line to the main program

    25 Basearea=0:V=0

and re-RUN the program. The values printed out for both these variables will be 0. This means that the same variable names can be used in both the main program and the function and can remain independent of each other, always provided they are either formal parameters or have been declared LOCAL within the function.

Note: Subprograms such as the user-defined functions discussed above, or the procedures and subroutines to be discussed shortly, are self-contained program units which can perform specific functions. If we observe certain guidelines it is possible to build up a library of standard subprograms, which can then be used as building blocks to assemble new, lengthier programs. The guidelines to be observed in this book are as follows:

All subprograms will be given 5-digit line numbers with the first two digits common to all lines of the subprogram, that is, 10000 to 10999 will be the line numbers of one subprogram, while 11000 to 11999 will be those of another. This point has been adhered to in the user-defined function given previously.

---------------------- **Problem 4.1** ----------------------
Modify the program given before so that it incorporates a second user-defined function which rounds, to the second decimal place, the calculated values for the volumes. Use the formula given under the INT() function with a value for D = 2.

Procedures

Procedures are in many ways similar to user-defined functions. However, the major difference between them is that, whereas functions return a value to the main program, procedures can be used to write information on the screen, the printer or the disk, as well as carry out complicated calculations which can be passed to the main program through global variables.

Thus, a procedure is a section of a program which is given a name and which can be called by name from any part of the program. After the procedure has been executed, program control is returned to the statement following the calling statement. The general form of a procedure which could be used to, say, calculate the sum of money returned on an investment, is written as follows:

    10000 DEF PROCInterest(Principal,Rate,Years)
        !
        !
        !
    10100 ENDPROC

To call this procedure from any part of the program, including from within the procedure itself, we must use the following call statement

    150 PROCInterest(A,B,C)

where variables A, B and C are the actual parameters. All the rules relating to actual and formal parameters, as well as global and local variables (discussed in the user-defined functions section) are applicable to procedures.

In Fig. 4.1 an example of the flow of a program incorporating a procedure is shown in diagrammatic form. When BASIC encounters the call statement PROCX in the main body of the program, it branches to the first statement of the procedure DEF PROCX, and continues to execute the statements within the subprogram until the ENDPROC statement is encountered. ENDPROC diverts the program flow to the statement immediately following the call statement.

Successive call statements can branch to the same procedure. Each time the ENDPROC statement is reached, the main program is resumed at the last call statement from which it branched.

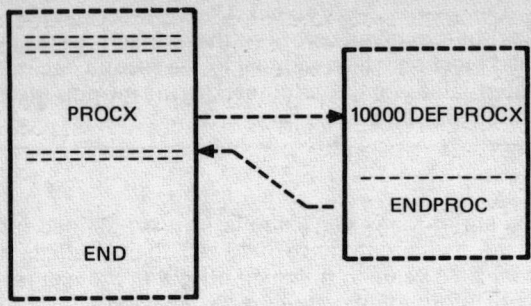

Fig. 4.1 Diagrammatic representation of program with procedure.

The following program, which calculates the compound interest on money lent, will be used to illustrate the use of procedures. The program calculates the compound interest using the formula

Amount = Principal*(1+Rate/100)^Years

where Principal is the money lent, and Amount is what it amounts to in time Years at Rate per cent per annum.

```
10 REM COMPOUND INTEREST
20 INPUT "AMOUNT LENT? " P
30 INPUT "INTEREST RATE? " R
40 INPUT "NUMBER OF YEARS? " N:PRINT
50 PRINT "YEARS";TAB(10);"INTEREST";TAB(26);
   "AMOUNT":PRINT
60 FOR Y=1 TO N
70    PROCInterest(P,R,Y)
80    Interest=Amount-P
90    PRINT TAB(0);Y;TAB(10);Interest;TAB(26);Amount
100 NEXT Y
110 END
10000 REM CALCULATE COMPOUND INTEREST
10010 DEF PROCInterest(Principal,Rate,Years)
10020 Amount=Principal*(1+Rate/100)^Years
10030 ENDPROC
```

After entering the investment parameters P, R and N, the procedure PROCInterest is called several times from within the FOR-NEXT loop set up in line 60. The parameters are passed to it at the same time through the argument list of the call statement. The values of these parameters are then used as the variables Principal, Rate and Years in the procedure. After executing all the statements within the procedure, program control passes back to line 80 in the main program where the value of Interest is calculated prior to PRINTing the results in line 90.

Type this program, SAVE it under the filename COMPINT and RUN it using the values of 5000, 11 and 15 for P, R and N respectively. A program RUN using these numbers is given below.

```
AMOUNT LENT? 5000
INTEREST RATE? 11
NUMBER OF YEARS? 15
```

YEARS	INTEREST	AMOUNT
1	550	5550
2	1160.5	6160.5
3	1838.155	6838.155
4	2590.35205	7590.35204
5	3425.29077	8425.29077
6	4352.07275	9352.07275
7	5380.80076	10380.8008
8	6522.68883	11522.6888
9	7790.1846	12790.1846
10	9197.10491	14197.1049
11	10758.7865	15758.7865
12	12492.253	17492.253
13	14416.4008	19416.4008
14	16552.2049	21552.2049
15	18922.9474	23922.9474

It is evident that the program works, showing the interest earned each year which is re-invested to give the final amout after 15 years. In most cases however only two decimal places are required when dealing with money. We will now use additional procedures to improve the appearance of the output.

By using the following procedure, numbers will be rounded to two digits after the decimal point.

```
11000 REM CONVERT NUMBERS TO $$$.$$ FORMAT
11010 DEF PROCRound
11020 Rounded=INT(10^Places*Number+0.5)/10^Places
11030 ENDPROC
```

The values of variables Places and Number are the decimal places required and the number to be rounded respectively. As the variable Rounded is not a formal parameter, any changes made to it will change its value anywhere within the program calling the procedure. By setting the value of Places and Number before calling the procedure, numbers can be rounded in any part of the main program.

Lines 75 and 85 following, when added to the main program, will initialize the value of Number and Places, call the procedure and then put the rounded values into the the appropriate variables for PRINTing in line 90.

```
75 Number=Amount:Places=2:PROCRound:
   Amount=Rounded
85 Number=Interest:Places=2:PROCRound:
   Interest=Rounded
```

Add these two lines, SAVE the program under the filename RCOMINT and re-RUN it. The output will now look as follows:

```
AMOUNT LENT 5000
INTEREST RATE 11
NUMBER OF YEARS 15
YEARS     INTEREST        AMOUNT
1         550             5550
2         1160.5          6160.5
3         1838.15         6838.15
4         2590.35         7590.35
5         3425.29         8425.29
6         4352.07         9352.07
7         5380.8          10380.8
8         6522.69         11522.69
9         7790.18         12790.18
10        9197.1          14197.1
11        10758.79        15758.79
12        12492.25        17492.25
13        14416.4         19416.4
14        16552.2         21552.2
15        18922.95        23922.95
```

Right-justifying numbers

Note that the results of the previous program are not right-justified, which makes it rather difficult, say, to add the figures in each column. The procedure given below will add any missing zeros after the decimal point and then right-justify all the numbers. We shall use it to illustrate further the use of procedures.

We have already said that procedures are self-contained program units which perform given functions. As such, they can be written and tested independently of the main program which is exactly what we have done below.

```
10 REM TEST PROGRAM FOR PROCRjustify
20 REM USE INTEGERS OR DECIMAL NUMBERS
30 REPEAT
40    INPUT "ENTER A NUMBER " N
50    Rounded=INT(10^2*N+.5)/10^2
60    PROCRjustify
70    PRINT Justified$
80 UNTIL N=0:END
```

```
12000 REM RIGHT-JUSTIFY NUMBERS
12010 DEF PROCRjustify
12020 LOCAL J:Z$=STR$(Rounded):Lengthz=LEN(Z$)
12030 FOR J=1 TO Lengthz:IF MID$(Z$,J,1)="." THEN
      LJ=J: L=Lengthz:NEXT J:GOTO 12060
12040 NEXT J
12050 Z$=Z$+".00":GOTO 12080
12060 IF (Lengthz-LJ)=2 GOTO 12080
12070 Z$=Z$+"0"
12080 Justified$=RIGHT$("          "+Z$,10)
12090 ENDPROC
```

SAVE this program under the filename JUSTIFY. The input parameter to this procedure is Rounded. As it is not a formal parameter, any changes to it in the procedure will change its value anywhere in the program. Line 12020 converts variable Rounded to a string and then makes Lengthz equal to the length of this string. Line 12030 searches the string for a decimal point and if it does not find one it concatenates to it the string '.00'. If, however, it finds a decimal point within the string, it jumps to line 12060 where it checks to see whether there are 2 digits after the decimal point or not. If there are, it jumps to line 12080, otherwise it concatenates one zero to the end of the string and goes to line 12080 where ten blank characters are concatenated, and the ten rightmost characters of the resulting string are assigned to Justified$.

This is important, because if Z$ were shorter than ten characters, then blank characters are required in front of it in order to provide the correct right-justification. If you have any difficulty in understanding what is going on here, you should look up the overlaying technique under 'concatenation' in Chapter 3.

---------- Problem 4.2 ----------

Modify the above program so that PROCRjustify can cater for numbers with any specified number of digits after the decimal point. This number is to be specified by the input parameter Places.

Note that one way of doing this is to change line 12050 so that the decimal point is concatenated first, followed by Places number of zeros. Similarly, lines 12060 to 12070 must now be changed so that the correct number of zeros are concatenated to the end of the string. These could vary in number from 1 to Places–1 zeros.

We shall now put together the RCOMINT program with the procedure, saved as JUSTIFY, developed above. The resulting program follows.

```
10 REM COMPOUND INTEREST (JUSTIFIED)
20 INPUT "AMOUNT LENT? " P
30 INPUT "INTEREST RATE? " R
40 INPUT "NUMBER OF YEARS? " N:PRINT
50 PRINT "YEARS";TAB(10);"INTEREST";TAB(26);
   "AMOUNT":PRINT
60 FOR Y=1 TO N
70   PROCInterest(P,R,Y)
75   Number=Amount:Places=2:PROCRound:
      Amount=Rounded:
      PROCRjustify:Amount$=Justified$
80   Interest=Amount-P
85   Number=Interest:Places=2:PROCRound:
     Interest=Rounded:
     PROCRjustify:Interest$=Justified$
88   Y$=STR$(Y):Y$=RIGHT$("         "+Y$,3)
90   PRINT TAB(0);Y$;TAB(8);Interest$;TAB(22);
     Amount$ 100 NEXT Y
110 END
10000 REM CALCULATE COMPOUND INTEREST
10010 DEF PROCInterest(Principal,Rate,Years)
10020 Amount=Principal*(1+Rate/100)^Years
10030 ENDPROC
11000 REM CONVERT NUMBERS TO $$$.$$ FORMAT
11010 DEF PROCRound
11020 Rounded=INT(10^Places*Number+0.5)/10^Places
11030 ENDPROC
12000 REM RIGHT-JUSTIFY NUMBERS
12010 DEF PROCRjustify
12020 LOCAL J:Z$=STR$(Rounded):Lengthz=LEN(Z$)
12030 FOR J=1 TO Lengthz:IF MID$(Z$,J,1)="."
        THEN LJ=J: J=Lengthz:NEXT J:GOTO 12060
12040 NEXT J
12050 Z$=Z$+".00":GOTO 12080
12060 IF (Lengthz-LJ)=2 GOTO 12080
12070 Z$=Z$+"0"
12080 Justified$=RIGHT$("         "+Z$,10)
12090 ENDPROC
```

Note the changes to lines 75, 85 and 90 and the addition of line 88 which allows justification of the year numbers. This later change could be achieved in several ways, the easiest being PROCRjustify. However its use would have resulted in year numbers with two decimal places. It would have been possible, of course, to have a separate procedure to deal with integers. However, since the logic does not have to be repeated frequently, we have chosen here to incorporate the required changes in the main program.

SAVE the program under the filename FCOMINT. On RUNning this final version, we get:

```
AMOUNT LENT 5000
INTEREST RATE 11
 NUMBER OF YEARS 15
YEARS       INTEREST        AMOUNT
  1            550.00         5550.00
  2           1160.50         6160.50
  3           1838.15         6838.15
  4           2590.35         7590.35
  5           3425.29         8425.29
  6           4352.07         9352.07
  7           5380.80        10380.80
  8           6522.69        11522.69
  9           7790.18        12790.18
 10           9197.10        14197.10
 11          10758.79        15758.79
 12          12492.25        17492.25
 13          14416.40        19416.40
 14          16552.20        21552.20
 15          18922.95        23922.95
```

Nested procedures

It is obvious from the listing of FCOMINT, that the program flow branches to procedure PROCInterest, and returns to the main program only to branch immediately to procedure PROCRound. Another way of achieving this would be first to branch to procedure PROCInterest, then prior to returning to the main program, branch to procedure PROCRound from within procedure PROCInterest.

In block form what we have done is as follows:

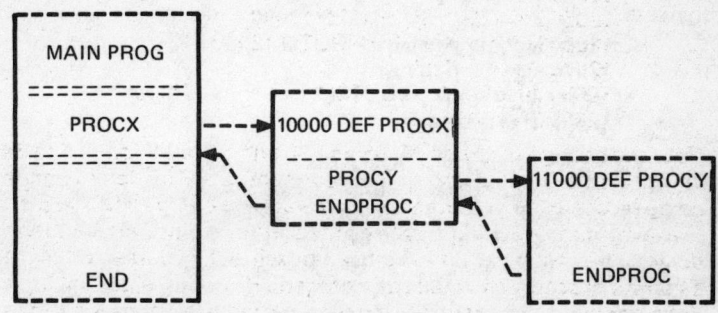

Fig. 4.2 Diagrammatic representation of nested procedure

Note the return path from procedure PROCY. It first returns to procedure PROCX and subsequently the ENDPROC statement within that procedure returns control to the main program. Procedure PROCY in the above configuration is known as a nested procedure. Procedures can even call themselves; the technique is then called recursion.

Recursion

Recursion is simply a means of letting a procedure call itself. This can lead to some very elegant and efficient programs. The program listed below can be used to provide a conversion table from one currency to another. It is recursive, with the procedure calling itself many times until the problem is completed. This program is worth studying as recursive programming can be a very powerful technique once it is understood.

```
10 REM CURRENCY CONVERSION (RECURSIVE)
20 INPUT "CURRENCY 1? " Currency1$
30 INPUT "CURRENCY 2? " Currency2$
40 INPUT "EXCHANGE RATE? " Rate
50 INPUT "MAXIMUM RANGE? " Max
60 PRINT:PRINT Currency1$,Currency2$
70 PROCConversion(Max): END
13000 DEF PROCConversion(Max)
13010 IF Max<1 THEN ENDPROC
13020 PROCConversion(Max-1)
13030 PRINT TAB(3);Max;TAB(11);Max*Rate
13040 ENDPROC
```

SAVE the program under the filename CONVERT. On RUNning it BASIC asks you to define CURRENCY 1 and CURRENCY 2, the EXCHANGE RATE and the MAXIMUM RANGE. On supplying the information shown below, BASIC calculates and PRINTs the answers.

```
CURRENCY 1? POUNDS
CURRENCY 2? DOLLARS
EXCHANGE RATE? 1.54
MAXIMUM RANGE? 10
```

POUNDS	DOLLARS
1	1.54
2	3.08
3	4.62
4	6.16
5	7.7
6	9.24
7	10.78
8	12.32
9	13.86
10	15.4

If we hadn't used recursion, we would have had to set up a loop to iterate through the range 1-10. By using recursion, we have broken the problem down into several simpler ones of printing up to the value of Max-1. This is repeated until Max-1 is less than one.

It is quite difficult to understand how the logic of a recursive procedure works at first. To illustrate the process, we shall look at the above example with Max=3. Fig. 4.3 shows the logic flow. Remember that, with procedures, program control returns to the statement after the last procedure call when an ENDPROC statement is reached.

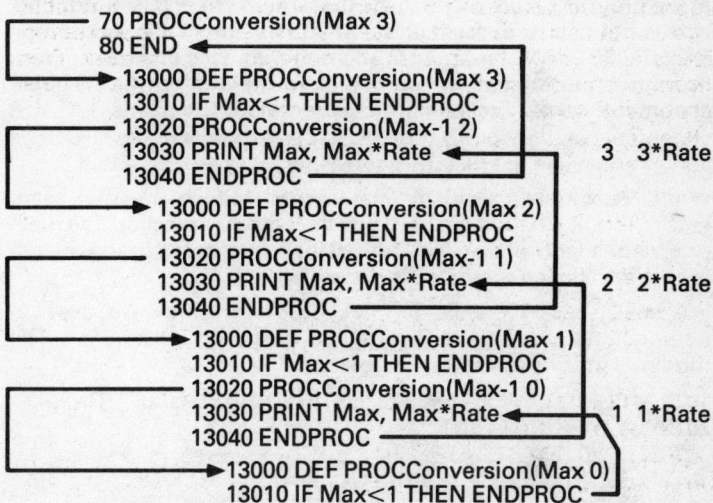

Fig. 4.3 Flow of logic in recursive procedures

After line 70 the program diverts to the DEF PROC line with Max set to 3. As Max is not less than 1, program control passes to line 13020 where the procedure is called again with Max=2. Once more control is passed to the DEF PROC statement after which there is another call to the procedure with Max=1. Finally, this is repeated with Max=0. At this point a change in the program flow takes place because Max is less than 1 so the last ENDPROC is executed. Line 13020 (the line after the last procedure call) is then reached and the first line of the table is printed. There is now another ENDPROC statement so the program jumps to the line following the previous procedure call and the second line of the table is printed. This is repeated once more before control passes to line 80 where program execution ends.

To print the conversion table in the reverse order, renumber line 13030 to 13015.

Subroutines

Subroutines are similar to procedures in many ways but they are not as powerful. They are supported by BBC-BASIC primarily because they are the only way that many other microcomputers can code frequently used sections of logic into subprograms. Thus, programs written for other versions of BASIC can be easily adapted to run under BBC-BASIC.

The GOSUB and RETURN statements

When BASIC encounters the GOSUB statement in the main body of the program, it branches to the first statement of the subroutine, and continues to execute the statements within the subroutine until the RETURN statement is encountered. This diverts program flow to the statement immediately following the GOSUB statement which called the subroutine. Thus, the GOSUB statement can be broadly thought to corresponds to the PROC call statement, while the RETURN corresponds to the ENDPROC.

When successive GOSUB statements branch to the same subroutine, each time the RETURN statement is reached, the main program is resumed at the last GOSUB statement from which it branched. No line reference is necessary.

We shall modify the FCOMPINT program which we used to demonstrate procedures in order to illustrate subroutines. The modified program is shown below.

```
10 REM COMPOUND INTEREST (JUSTIFIED WITH SUBROUTINES)
20 INPUT "AMOUNT LENT? " P
30 INPUT "INTEREST RATE? " R
40 INPUT "NUMBER OF YEARS? " N:PRINT
50 PRINT "YEARS";TAB(10);"INTEREST";TAB(26);
   "AMOUNT":PRINT
60 FOR Y=1 TO N
70    SPrincipal=P:SRate=R:SYears=Y:GOSUB 10000
      :Amount=SAmount
75    SNumber=Amount:SPlaces=2:SC=10:GOSUB 11000:
      Amount=SRounded:GOSUB 12000:Amount$=SJustified$
80    Interest=Amount-P
85    SNumber=Interest:SPlaces=2:SC=10:GOSUB 11000:
      GOSUB 12000:Interest$=SJustified$
88    SC=3:Z$=STR$(Y):GOSUB 12080:Y$=SJustified$
90    PRINT TAB(0);Y$;TAB(8);Interest$;TAB(22);Amount$
100 NEXT Y
110 END
10000 REM CALCULATE COMPOUND INTEREST
10010 REM INPUT Param: SPrincipal,SRate,SYears;
      OUTPUT Param:SAmount
10020 SAmount=SPrincipal*(1+SRate/100)^SYears
10030 RETURN
```

```
11000 REM CONVERT NUMBERS TO $$$.$$ FORMAT
11010 REM INPUT Param: SNumber,SPlaces;
      OUTPUT Param:SRounded
11020 SRounded=INT(10^SPlaces*SNumber+0.5)/10^SPlaces
11030 RETURN
12000 REM RIGHT-JUSTIFY NUMBERS
12010 REM INPUT Param: SRounded,SC; OUTPUT Param: SJustified$
12020 Z$=STR$(SRounded):Lengthz=LEN(Z$)
12030 FOR J=1 TO Lengthz:IF MID$(Z$,J,1)="." THEN LJ=J:
      J=Lengthz:NEXT J:GOTO 12060
12040 NEXT J
12050 Z$=Z$+".00":GOTO 12080
12060 IF (Lengthz-LJ)=2 GOTO 12080
12070 Z$=Z$+"0"
12080 SJustified$=RIGHT$("     "+Z$,SC)
12090 RETURN
```

After entering the investment parameters P, R and N, the first subroutine is called several times from within the FOR-NEXT loop set up in line 60. The parameters of the subroutine are initialized by the first three statements in line 70. Note that we have prefixed all subroutine parameters with the letter S to distinguish them from other variables. After executing all the statements within the subroutine, program control passes back to the statement following the GOSUB in the main program (in this case the last statement of line 70). Following lines call other subroutines.

SAVE this program under the filename FCOMSUB, and then RUN it to verify that you get the same results as before. You will notice that the program takes longer to run. Procedures are faster than the equivalent subroutines.

Programs can be written to incorporate nested subroutines in the same way as procedures, although recursion in not possible. However, we shall not pursue this subject any further as the whole point of BBC-BASIC is its ability to code subprograms as procedures, thus avoiding the messy logic one could get into by using subroutines.

Appendix A
Debugging Techniques

There are several techniques at a programmer's disposal which can be used to isolate program errors (known as bugs). Such bugs can be introduced into a program either while typing the program into the computer by pressing the wrong keys, or through bad logic. We shall examine both these cases and indicate suitable techniques for debugging programs.

Syntax errors
This type of error is reported when part of an instruction cannot be understood by the computer. A few of these errors reveal themselves immediately the RETURN key is pressed but most are not discovered until the program is executed. To illustrate both of these, type the following lines with the indicated (underlined) errors.

> 100 REN... DEBUGGING EXAMPLE...
> 200 INPUT "WEIGHT? " TONS
> 300300 PRINT "WEIGHT IS ";TONS

Immediately after pressing RETURN, following the last line, BASIC will respond with

> Too big

which is caused by the high line number (300 typed twice). Retype the line as follows:

> 300 PRINT "WEIGHT IS ";TONS

On RUNning this program, BASIC will respond with

> Silly at line 100

and on LISTing 100 you will be confronted with

> 100 RENUMBER.. DEBUGGING EXAMPLE...

Because REN was typed instead of REM, line 100 was not recognised as a REMark statement. Furthermore, REN. has been interpreted as the shortened version of the RENUMBER command and has been printed accordingly in full. RENUMBER.. is not understood by BASIC and so the error message was printed on the screen.

Retype line 100 correctly (REM) and re-RUN the program. On execution, BASIC asks for an input and immediately prints

> Syntax error at line 200

The reason for this message is not so easy to see. TONS has been used as a variable, but the BASIC interpreter has treated the initial two letters as the keyword TO. As it cannot understand the statement TO NS, the error message is produced. To overcome this problem, retype the line with the variable called Tons and then re-RUN the program. A further error message

    Syntax error at line 300

is produced because we have asked the computer to PRINT the variable TONS, which does not exist, in line 300. Finally, changing TONS to Tons in line 300 results in a working program.

Syntax errors can usually be spotted easily although some of them cause problems. For example, it is easy to misread program listings and hence type "l" (lower case L) instead of "1" or "O" (upper case o) instead of "0" (zero). Errors in logic are often much harder to trace.

Logic errors

Errors resulting from bad logic can cause much wasted time unless you learn to trace systematically through your programs. Such errors can cause the program to crash or lead to totally unexpected results. Occasionally, the error will cause the system to 'hang' so that you cannot use the keyboard to type a command or to get a response from the ESCAPE key. As an example of this, RUN the following two line program:

    10 ON ERROR CRASH
    20 ERROR

The computer will not accept any keyboard entries and the ESCAPE key won't work. Rebooting the computer by pressing CTRL ALT DEL is the only way out in this case. If a long program causes this to happen, all values held in variables and possibly the program itself would be lost.

To trace logic errors effectively is is necessary to go though the program with pencil and paper actually working out the results you would expect. You can then step through the program in the computer to see if the same results are being obtained.

The TRACE command is used to see if program flow is following the paths expected. LOAD any program and then type

    TRACE ON

prior to RUNning it. This will cause the printing on the screen of all the line numbers of the statements as they are being executed. You can thus trace the program to the area in which trouble begins. Line numbers appear on the screen in square brackets. The TRACE command will be cancelled if you type

        TRACE OFF

or if you press the ESCAPE key, or if an error is encountered.

If the logic of part of a program is to be TRACEd, the TRACE ON and TRACE OFF commands can be given line numbers and be included in the program. Frequently, the programmer wants to TRACE the logic of the main program but not the procedures or subroutines. If these are given high line numbers, as suggested in this book, then the main program only will be traced by using

        TRACE 1000   (or any other suitable number)

Only lines below 1000 will now be traced.

When the program fails it is often useful to know the value of the variable used up to that point. These can be found by PRINTing them out. For example, the error message

        No such variable at line 150

is not completely clear if line 150 is

        150 PRINT A,B(5),C,D

To find the variable concerned, it is necessary to PRINT each one in turn.

Many computer languages allow the programmer to STOP a program during its execution, PRINT out the values of selected variables and then continue. BBC-BASIC does not allow this. However, the problem can be easily overcome with the use of the following procedure.

```
30000 DEF PROCTest(N)
30010 REPEAT:PRINT "PROCTEST ";N
30020 LOCAL V$
30030 INPUT "VARIABLE TO BE PRINTED? " V$
30040 IF V$<>"" THEN PRINT EVAL(V$):UNTIL V$=""
30050 ENDPROC
```

This procedure is written with high line numbers so that it will not interfere with any other procedures which might be used in the program. By including the statements PROCTest(1), PROCTest(2) etc. at suitable points in the program, control will be transferred to the procedure and the message

        PROCTEST 1
        VARIABLE TO BE PRINTED?

will appear on the screen. Entering any valid variable causes its value to be printed. Pressing RETURN without entering a variable makes the program continue until the next PROCTest is reached.

Common causes of errors

Misprints
- l instead of numeral 1
- . instead of ,   (often in DATA statements)
- O instead of numeral 0   (severe problems in DATA lines)
- , instead of ;   (often in VDU statements)

Spaces
- IF A=BTHEN...   (BTHEN treated as a variable)
- FOR X=ATOB...   (ATOB treated as a variable)
- PRINTTAB (5)   (There must not be spaces between TAB and the opening bracket)

Reserved words
- TONS=X;PRINT TONS   (Upper case variables must not start with a BASIC keyword. If not sure, use lower case letters for all but first letter of long variables)

Appendix B
Representation of Numeric Data

Binary representation

Numeric information is stored in computers in the form of groups of binary digits (bits for short), i.e. 0 and 1. In almost all present day computers information is structured in groups of 8 bits (called a byte). Numbers can be represented in direct binary format in which the right-most bit represents 2 to the power of 0; the next one to the left, 2 to the power of 1; the next one, 2 to the power of 2; and so on, until we reach the left-most bit which is 2 to the power of 7 for an 8 bit structure. This can be represented as follows:

$$2^7 + 2^6 + 2^5 + 2^4 + 2^3 + 2^2 + 2^1 + 2^0$$

A binary number can be converted to its equivalent decimal by multiplying the value of the appropriate Ith bit (which can be either 0 or 1) with the result of 2^I. For example, the binary number 0001 0101 is equivalent to $(0*128) + (0*64) + (0*32) + (1*16) + (0*8) + (1*4) + (0*2) + (1*1) = 21$ decimal.

It can easily be shown that with n bits available, integer numbers within the range 0 to (2^n-1) can be represented. Therefore,

> 4 bits (called a nibble) can represent the range 0-15
> 8 bits (called a byte) can represent the range 0-255
> 16 bits (two bytes) can represent the range 0-65535.

Note the special case of 10 binary digits which give a maximum of 1024 decimal numbers (0-1023). We represent this by the symbol K so that a 512K computer has $(512*1024-1)=524,287$ memory locations available.

The following program gives the whole binary sequence for a given number of bits.

```
10 REM BINARY SEQUENCE GENERATOR
20 INPUT "ENTER NUMBER OF BITS " N
30 Decimax=2^N-1:PRINT:PRINT "MAX DECIMAL NR IN ";
   N;" BITS = ";Decimax:PRINT
40 PRINT TAB(5);"DECIM. NR";TAB(21);"BINARY NR":PRINT
50 FOR Count=0 TO Decimax:Bits$="":Temp=Count
60    FOR I=1 TO N:Value=Temp/2:Ival=INT(Value):
         IF (Value-Ival) < 0.001 THEN T$="0":GOTO 80
70       T$="1"
80       Temp=Ival:Bits$=T$+Bits$:NEXT I
90    PRINT Count;TAB(21);Bits$
100 NEXT Count:END
```

Type this program and RUN it. Try it with 2, 4 and 8 bits to see how decimal numbers are represented in binary. If you have about 4 hours to spare, try the program with 16 bits. Remember, there are going to be a total of 65,536 possible combinations of 0s and 1s in 16 bits.

The IBM and compatible computer's microprocessor is capable of addressing a maximum of 640 KBytes of memory starting from location 0 and extending to location 655,359. Of these, 600K are available to the user, the rest being used by the system itself. By comparison, the equivalent figures for the BBC computer are 64K maximum available memory (plus another 64K in shadow RAM for the Master series) of which only 32K are available to the user.

Hexadecimal representation

Most operations done by the computer are carried out in binary and although this is easily understood by the computer it causes problems for mere mortals. For example, the address of memory location 65535 in decimal, is 1111111111111111. Sixteen bits are required to represent all the storage addresses and it is very easy to make mistakes when working with this many digits. The hexadecimal numbering system, or hex for short, is used to overcome some of these difficulties.

The hex counting system uses base 16 as opposed to base 10 in the decimal and base 2 in binary system. Counting in 16's is difficult at first, but it does have advantages as you will see later. The value of each column with the different number systems is shown below.

Value of one unit in column

	Col 4	Col 3	Col 2	Col 1
Binary	2^3	2^2	2^1	2^0
	(8)	(4)	(2)	(1)
Decimal	10^3	10^2	10^1	10^0
	(1000)	(100)	(10)	(1)
Hexadecimal	16^3	16^2	16^1	16^0
	(4096)	(256)	(16)	(1)

The Hex system requires 16 different digits compared with 10 and 2 in the other systems. It uses 0-9 as in decimal, plus the letters A-F. A list of the first sixteen numbers in each system follows.

Binary	Decimal	Hexadecimal
0000	00	0
0001	01	1
0010	02	2
0011	03	3
0100	04	4
0101	05	5
0110	06	6
0111	07	7
1000	08	8
1001	09	9
1010	10	A
1011	11	B
1100	12	C
1101	13	D
1110	14	E
1111	15	F

An example, converting a hexadecimal number to a decimal number, will make things clearer. BASIC programs on BBC computers start from memory location 0E00(hex) on machines not fitted with a disk interface. The decimal equivalent of this number is given by

```
  0 (which is decimal 0)  * 4096 =    0
+ E (which is decimal 14) *  256 = 3584
+ 0 (which is decimal 0)  *   16 =    0
+ 0 (which is decimal 0)  *    1 =    0
                                   ─────
                                    3584
```

Hex numbers can be used when programming in BBC-BASIC as long as the computer knows that they are in hex. The ampersand sign (&) is used to do this. Any number preceeded by & is treated as a hex number. Thus, &110 is the hex equivalent of decimal 272.

Whilst in immediate mode, the conversion between hex and decimal can be done very easily using the tilde (~) and ampersand signs.

 PRINT &FFFF gives the decimal 65535, while
 PRINT ~65535 gives the hex FFFF

If you have many numbers to convert, use the program DEC-HEX given below. On RUNning the program you will be asked to enter a decimal number. After entering the number, the hex equivalent will be printed. Switching from decimal to hex modes and vice versa is achieved by pressing RETURN without entering any data.

```
10 REM HEX-DEC AND DEC-HEX CONVERTER
20 REPEAT:REPEAT
30   PRINT:INPUT "ENTER DECIMAL NUMBER " N
40   IF N<>0 THEN PRINT "HEX EQUIVALENT IS ";~N
50 UNTIL N=0
60 REPEAT
70   PRINT:INPUT "ENTER HEX NUMBER " N$
80   IF N$<>"" THEN PRINT "DECIMAL EQUIVALENT IS ";
     EVAL("&"+N$)
90 UNTIL N$=""
100 UNTIL FALSE
```

The hexadecimal numbering system has an advantage over binary as one hex digit is equivalent to four binary digits. Thus, any 8-bit byte of memory can be represented by two hex digits, and any memory address (which requires twenty binary digits) by five hex digits.

Because of the advantage of hex over both binary and decimal systems, it is used for many computing applications. Although it is not necessary to use the hex system in BASIC programs (apart from using the @% variable in PRINT formatting – see Appendix C), it is essential to understand it if you want to learn assembly language programming.

Appendix C
Print Formatting

The PRINT statement is used to print words and numbers on the screen and also on paper if a printer is connected and enabled. It is followed by a print list which is a list of items to be printed, each item being separated from the next by special punctuation which formats the layout to be produced. Punctuation marks used are the comma (,), the apostrophe ('), the semicolon (;) and quotation marks (''). How these are used is shown below.

Print list items in quotation marks are printed, in the next available print position, exactly as they appear in the list. String variables are printed in the same way, but numbers and numeric variables are right justified in their print fields. The screen is divided into vertical strips or fields which are initially 10 characters wide. This can be altered by the @% variable which is described below. By the use of punctuation, printing is forced to occur at the next position or in the next field.

> The comma — A comma after an item causes the rest of the current field to be filled with spaces. The following item will be printed in the next field.
>
> The semicolon   This causes the following item in the print list to be printed in the next print position (no gap left).
>
> The apostrophe   An apostrophe in a print list causes the cursor to move to the next line before anything else is printed.

Changing the format: The @% variable
This variable is used to produce a wide variety of print formats. The print field width, the number of decimal places and the number of figures printed can be controlled solely by changing the value of @%.

The @% variable is a four byte variable which is most easily understood in its hex form (see Appendix B). We will number the bytes, from the left, as B4, B3, B2 and B1. These bytes are examined in turn, starting from B4, to set the print format.

> B4   This byte is tested by the function STR$(). If B4 is 0 the rest of the number is ignored. If it is 1, strings will be formatted, by the STR$() function, according to the setting of @%.

B3   This byte is used to select the basic format.

Value of B3
&00   General or G format. Integers will be printed as integers. Other numbers, greater than 0.1, are printed as normal, while numbers less than 0.1 are printed in exponent format.

&01   Exponent or E format. Numbers are always printed in scientific notation. Thus, 100 is 1E2, 1500 is 1.5E3 and —0.015 is —1.5E-2.

&02   Fixed or F format. Numbers are printed with a fixed number of decimal places. Decimal points are aligned vertically as with normal accounting procedure. If the number cannot fit into the field width selected, it reverts to the G format.

B2   This byte controls the number of digits printed. If it is too large or small for the mode used, it is taken as 10 or &0A. Its effect depends on the format used.

G format   B2 gives the maximum number of digits which can be printed before reverting to E format. The value ranges from 1-10 (&01 to &0A).

E format   B2 gives the total number of digits, excluding the decimal point, which can be printed before the E part of the number. Its value ranges from 1-10 (&01 to &0A).

F format   B2 specifies the number of digits to follow the decimal point. It ranges from 0-10 (&00 to &0A).

B1   This byte controls the field width which can vary from 0 to 255. In hex this is &00 to &FF.

If an overall field width of 12 characters with 3 decimal places in fixed format is required, the @% variable would be calculated as follows: Assume that strings created by the STR$() function are also to be formatted this way.

	B4	B3	B2	B1
STR$() formatting required	01			
Fixed format		02		
3 decimal places			03	
12 character field (12=&C)				0C
	01	02	03	0C

By typing, in immediate mode, @%=&0102030C, or including this as a line in a program, output will be formatted as required. The leading 0 can be left out. To set the print format back to its General form with a field width of 10, set @%=&10.

Solutions to Problems

The solutions to the problems presented in this Appendix as well as all the programs in the text can be purchased on disk by writing to the authors at the Camborne School of Mines, Redruth, Cornwall, TR15 3SE.

Problem 1.1
```
10 REM AVERAGES
20 A=26.9
30 B=28.2
40 C=27.3
50 D=A+B+C
60 X=D/3
70 PRINT "VALUES:";SPC(5);"A";SPC(5);"B";SPC(5);"C";
   SPC(5);"AVERAGE"
80 PRINT TAB(10);A;TAB(16);B;TAB(22);C;TAB(28);X
90 END
```

Problem 1.2
```
10 REM TEMPERATURE CONVERSION
20 INPUT "ENTER VALUE " F
30 C=(F-32)*5/9
40 PRINT SPC(1);F;"DEGREES F=";SPC(1);C;" DEGREES C"
50 END
```

Problem 1.3
```
10 REM TIME CONVERSION
20 PRINT "DAYS","HOURS","MINUTES","TOTAL MIN"
30 READ Days,Hours,Minutes
40 DATA 2,10,30
50 Total=Days*24*60+Hours*60+Minutes
60 PRINT TAB(0);Days;TAB(10);Hours;TAB(20);Minutes;
   TAB(30);Total
70 END
```

Problem 1.4
```
10 REM PRIORITIES
20 READ A,B,C,D,E,F,G
30 DATA 5,3,8,4,7,2,6
40 X1=A*B^E+F
50 X2=A*B^(E+F)
60 X3=A*B/C*D
70 X4=A*B/(C*D)
80 X5=A+B*G+C*G^2+D*G^3
90 X6=(A+B)*G+C*G^2+D*G^3
100 X7=(A^F+(B-1/C)^F)^0.5
110 X8=(A^F+B-1/C^F)^0.5
120 X9=A/B^2-C*D/((E+F)+G^3)
130 PRINT TAB(1);"X1";TAB(14);"X2";TAB(28);"X3"
140 PRINT TAB(1);X1;TAB(14);X2;TAB(28);X3
150 PRINT TAB(1);"X4";TAB(14);"X5";TAB(28);"X6"
160 PRINT TAB(1);X4;TAB(14);X5;TAB(28);X6
170 PRINT TAB(1);"X7";TAB(14);"X8";TAB(28);"X9"
180 PRINT TAB(1);X7;TAB(14);X8;TAB(28);X9
190 END
```

Problem 2.1
```
10 REM THREE NUMBER SORT
15 REPEAT
20   INPUT "ENTER THREE NUMBERS " A,B,C:IF A=0
     THEN END
30   IF A<B THEN T=A:A=B:B=T
40   IF B<C THEN T=B:B=C:C=T:GOTO 30
50   PRINT A,B,C
52   PRINT
55 UNTIL FALSE
60 END
```

Problem 2.2

```
10 REM IMPERIAL TO MKS CONVERSION
20 READ A,B,C
30 DATA 4.54609,0.3048,0.453592
40 REPEAT:PRINT
50   INPUT "GALLONS/FEET/POUNDS/QUIT (1/2/3/4)" X:PRINT
60   ON X GOTO 80,120,160,70
70   END
80   INPUT "ENTER NR OF GALLONS " Gallons
90   Litres=A*Gallons
100  PRINT Gallons;" GALLONS = ";Litres;" LITRES"
110 UNTIL FALSE
120 INPUT "ENTER NR OF FEET " Feet
130 Metres=B*Feet
140 PRINT Feet;" FEET = ";Metres;" METRES"
150 UNTIL FALSE
160 INPUT "ENTER NR OF POUNDS " Pounds
170 Kilos=C*Pounds
180 PRINT Pounds;" POUNDS = ";Kilos;" KILOS"
190 UNTIL FALSE
```

Problem 2.3

```
10 REM SQUARE X
20 CLS:PRINT TAB(0,5)
30 FOR I=1 TO 15
40   PRINT TAB(11);
50   FOR J=1 TO 15
60     PRINT "X";
70   NEXT J
80   PRINT
90 NEXT I
100 END
```

Problem 2.4

```
10 REM BIG E
20 CLS
30 FOR I=1 TO 10:PRINT "EE";
40   IF I<3 OR I>8 THEN PRINT "EEEEEEE":GOTO 70
50   IF I=5 OR I=6 THEN PRINT "EEE":GOTO 70
60   PRINT
70 NEXT I
80 END
```

Problem 3.1(A)

Changes or additions to STOCK program are marked with asterisks.

```
*10 REM STOCKTAKING (A)
 20 DIM Item$(4),Stock$(4)
 30 FOR I=1 TO 4:READ Item$(I),Stock$(I):NEXT I
 40 REPEAT:PRINT
 50    INPUT "WHICH ITEM? " Name$
 60    IF Name$="END" THEN END
 70    FOR I=1 TO 4
*80       IF LEFT$(Item$(I),3)<>Name$ GOTO 100
 90       PRINT " >>>>>> ";LEFT$(Stock$(I),3);
          "IN STOCK AT $"; RIGHT$(Stock$(I),4);" EACH"
 100   NEXT I
 110 UNTIL FALSE
 120 DATA "INK ERASER","200,0.10"
 130 DATA "PENCIL ERASER","320,0.15"
 140 DATA "TYPING ERASER","25 ,0.25"
 150 DATA "CORRECTION FLUID","150,0.50"
```

Problem 3.1(B)

Changes or additions to STOCKA program are marked with asterisks

```
*10 REM STOCKTAKING (B)
*20 DIM Item$(4)
*30 FOR I=1 TO 4:READ Item$(I):NEXT I
 40 REPEAT:PRINT
 50    INPUT "WHICH ITEM? " Name$
 60    IF Name$="END" THEN END
 70    FOR I=1 TO 4
 80       IF LEFT$(Item$(I),3)<>Name$ GOTO 100
*90       PRINT ">>>>>> ";LEFT$(Item$(I),16); " ";
          MID$(Item$(I),18,3);" IN STOCK AT $";
          RIGHT$(Item$(I),4);" EACH"
 100   NEXT I
 110 UNTIL FALSE
*120 DATA "INK ERASER        ,200,0.10"
*130 DATA "PENCIL ERASER     ,320,0.15"
*140 DATA "TYPING ERASER     ,25 ,0.25"
*150 DATA "CORRECTION FLUID,150,0.50"
```

Problem 3.2
```
10 REM FIBONACCI SERIES
20 INPUT "HOW MANY TERMS? " N
30 DIM A(N),B(N-1):A(1)=1:A(2)=1
40 FOR I=3 TO N
50   A(I)=A(I-2)+A(I-1)
60 NEXT I:REM ALL TERMS STORED IN A()
70 FOR I=1 TO N-1
80   B(I)=(A(I)+A(I+1))/2
90 NEXT I:REM AVERAGES STORED IN B()
100 PRINT "F. SERIES";SPC(10);"AVERAGES"
110 FOR I=1 TO N:PRINT SPC(5);A(I);:IF I<>N THEN
    PRINT SPC(13);B(I)
120 NEXT I:PRINT:END
```

Problem 3.3
```
10 REM SPECIFY NUMBER/LETTER TO PRINT
     LETTER/NUMBER
20 REPEAT
30   PRINT "1. SPECIFY NUMBER TO PRINT LETTER"
40   PRINT "2. SPECIFY LETTER TO PRINT NUMBER"
50   PRINT "3. END PROGRAM"
60   REPEAT:PRINT:INPUT "CHOOSE (1/2/3) " Which
70   UNTIL Which >0 AND Which <4
80   ON Which GOTO 100,130,90
90   END
100   REPEAT:INPUT "ENTER NUMBER BETWEEN
      1 AND 26 " Number
110   UNTIL Number>0 AND Number<27
120   PRINT CHR$(64+Number):PRINT:UNTIL FALSE
130 REPEAT:INPUT "ENTER A LETTER " Letter$
140 UNTIL ASC(Letter$)>63 AND ASC(Letter$)<91
150 PRINT ASC(Letter$)-64:PRINT:UNTIL FALSE
```

Problem 3.4

Changes or additions to BUBBLE program are marked with asterisks

```
    10 REM BUBBLE SORT
    20 READ N: DIM Employee$(N)
    30 FOR I=1 TO N: READ Employee$(I): NEXT I
*32 REPEAT:INPUT "OUTPUT TO SCREEN OR
       PRINTER? (S/P) " Q$
*34 UNTIL Q$="S" OR Q$="P"
*36 IF LEFT$(Q$,1)="P" THEN VDU2
   40 FOR I=1 TO N:PRINT Employee$(I):NEXT I
   50 PRINT: PRINT: PRINT "SORTED INFORMATION"
   90 M=N
  100 FOR J=1 TO N-1
  105   M=M-1:Flag=0
  110   FOR I=1 TO M
  120     IF Employee$(I)> Employee$(I+1) THEN Flag=1:
            Temporary$=Employee$(I+1):Employee$ (I+1)=
            Employee$(I): Employee$(I)=Temporary$
  130   NEXT I
  140   PRINT: PRINT: PRINT TAB(0);J
  150   FOR I=1 TO N: PRINT Employee$(I): NEXT I
  160   Key$=GET$
  170   IF Flag=0 GOTO 400
  180 NEXT J
  300 DATA 5
  310 DATA "WILSON M. ,ROOM 1.24, 395"
  320 DATA "SMITH M.   ,ROOM 2.6 ,7315"
  330 DATA "JONES B.M.,ROOM 6.19,1698"
  340 DATA "SMITH A.A. ,ROOM 2.12, 456"
  350 DATA "BROWN C.   ,ROOM 3.1 , 432"
*400 PRINT:VDU3:END
```

Problem 4.1

Changes or additions to VOLUME program are marked with asterisks

```
   10 REM MULTI-LINE USER-DEFINED FUNCTION
   20 REM VOLUME OF A CYLINDER
   30 INPUT "RADIUS OF CYLINDER? " Radius
   40 INPUT "HEIGHT OF CYLINDER? " Height
   50 PRINT "VOLUME=";FNVolume(Radius,Height)
   60 END
10000 DEF FNVolume(R,H)
10010 Basearea=PI*R^2
10020 V=Basearea*H
*10025 Vround=FNRound(V)
*10030 =Vround
*11000 DEF FNRound(Num)=INT(Num*10^2+0.5)/100
```

Problem 4.2
Changes or additions to JUSTIFY program are marked with asterisks

```
  10 REM TEST PROGRAM FOR PROCRjustify
  20 REM USE INTEGERS OR DECIMAL NUMBERS
  30 REPEAT
  40   INPUT "ENTER A NUMBER " N
 *45   INPUT "ENTER NUMBER OF DECIMAL
       PLACES " Places
 *50   Rounded=INT(10^Places*N+.5)/10^Places
  60   PROCRjustify
  70   PRINT Justified$
  80 UNTIL N=0:END
12000 REM RIGHT-JUSTIFY NUMBERS
12010 DEF PROCRjustify
12020 LOCAL J:Z$=STR$(Rounded):Lengthz=LEN(Z$)
12030 FOR J=1 TO Lengthz:IF MID$(Z$,J,1)="." THEN
      LJ=J:J=Lengthz:NEXT J:GOTO 12060
12040 NEXT J
*12050 Z$=Z$+"."
*12052 FOR Zero=1 TO Places
*12054   Z$=Z$+"0"
*12056 NEXT Zero
*12060 IF (Lengthz-LJ)=Places GOTO 12080
*12070 REM
12080 Justified$=RIGHT$("          "+Z$,10)
12090 ENDPROC
```

Index

ABS() Function 53, 55
ACS() Function 53, 54
Alphabetical
  Comparison of Strings 35
  Sorting 47
AND statement 24
Arithmetic
  Functions 53
  Integer 10
  Operators 7
  Priority 18, 19
Arrays 37, 41
  Errors 43
ASC() Function 44
ASN() Function 53, 54
ASCII 35
  conversion codes 36
Assignment Statement 9, 20
ATN() Function 53, 54

BBC-BASIC86 1
Binary representation 77, 79
Block Diagrams 62, 67
Branching 21
Bubble sort 50
Byte 1, 77

Catalogue Directory Command (*.) 5
CHR$() Function 44
Clear Screen 14
CLS Statement 14
Computed GOTO Statement 25
Concatenation 35, 45
Constants 9, 10
COS() Function 53, 54
CTRL B command 1
CTRL C Command 1
CTRL N Command 1
CTRL O Command 1
CTRL SHIFT 1, 43

Data Sorting 24
DATA Statement 16
Debugging Techniques 73

Decimal Numbers
  to ASCII Conversion 36
  to Hex or Binary Conversion 77
DEF FN () Statement 59
Deferred Mode 8
Defined Functions 58
DEG() Function 53
*DEL Command 4, 5
Derived Functions 58
DIM Statement 37, 42
Disk
  Directory 5
  Filing System 4
*DIR Command 5
DIV 11
*DRIVE Command 5

Editing Screen 3
END Statement 2, 8
ENDPROC 61
EVAL() Function 45
*EXEC Command 5
EXP() Function 53, 55
Exponential Numbers 10
Expressions 11

Floating Point Numbers 10
FOR-NEXT Statement 26
Formatted PRINT 13, 31, 81
Functions
  ABS() 53, 55
  ACS() 53, 54
  ASC() 44
  ASN() 53, 54
  ATN() 53, 54
  COS() 53, 54
  DEG() 53
  EVAL() 45
  EXP() 53, 55
  INT() 53, 55
  LEN() 44
  LN() 53, 55

LOG() 53, 55
RAD() 53
RND() 53, 56
SGN() 53, 55
SIN() 53, 54
SQR() 53, 54
TAN() 53, 54
VAL() 45
Derived 58
User-Defined 58

GET$ Statement 49
Global Variables 60
GOSUB-RETURN Statement 70
GOTO Statement 21
  Computed 25

Headings 12
*HELP Command 5
Hexadecimal Notation 78
Hexadecimal to Decimal
  conversion 79

IF statement 21
  Logical Operators 23
IF THEN ELSE Statement 23
Immediate Mode 7
INPUT Statement 15
INT() Function 53, 55
Integer
  Arithmetic 11
  Numbers 10

Jump out of loops 30, 33
Justifying numbers 64

*KEY Command 5
Keyboard 1

LEFT$() Function 38
LEN() Function 44
LIST Command 4
Literals 35
LN() Function 53, 55
LOAD Command 4

LOCAL variables 60
LOG Conversion 55
LOG() Function 53, 55
Logical Operators 23
Loop Configurations 30

Memory ROM 1
MID$() Function 39
MOD 11
Mode
  Deferred 8
  Immediate 7
MODE Command 2
Multiple Statements on
  one line 38

Nested
  FOR-NEXT Loops 29
  PROCedures 67
NEW Command 12
Numeric Data Representation 77

OLD 12
OR Statement 24

Parameters
  in Functions 59
  in PROCedures 61
  in Subroutines 70
PRINT Statement 7, 8
  CHR$() 44
  with SPC 13
  with TAB 13
Printer
  connection 5, 51
  disconnection 6, 51
Priority, Arithmetic 18
PROC 61
Procedures 61
  Nested 67
  Recursive 68

RAD() Function 53
Random Numbers 56
READ Statement 16
Real Variables 9, 11
Recursion 68
REM Statement 12
*REN Command 4, 5
REPEAT- UNTIL loop 21
Reserved Words 10
Resident Integer Variables 11
RESTORE Statement 17
RETURN
  Key 2
  Statement 70
RIGHT$() Function 39
RND() Function 53, 56
ROM 1
Rounding Numbers 55, 56
RUN Command 8

SAVE Command 3
SGN() Function 53, 55
SHIFT Key 1
SIN() Function 53, 54
Sorting
  Alphabetic 47
  Bubble sort technique 50
  Data 24
SPC() Function 13
*SPOOL Command 5
SQR() Function 53, 54
STEP Modifier 28
STR$() Function 44
String 35
  Arrays 37
  Concatenation 35, 45
  Functions 38
    ASC() 44
    CHR$() 44
    EVAL() 45
    LEFT$() 38
    LEN() 44
    MID$() 39
    RIGHT$() 39
    STR$() 44
    VAL() 45
  Variables 35
Sub-Programs 53
  Functions 53, 58
    Single Line 59
    Multi-line 59
  PROCedures 61
    Nested 67
    Parameters 59, 61
    Recursive 68
  Subroutines 70
    Parameters 70
Subscripted Variables 41

TAB() Function 13
Tabulations 13
TAN() Function 53, 54
TIME Function 57
TRACE Command 74

User-Defined
  Functions 58

VAL() Function 45
Variables 9
    Global 60
    Integer 11
    LOCAL 60
    Real 11
    String 35
    Subscripted 41

VDU2 Command 5, 51
VDU3 Command 6, 51

Notes

Notes

Notes

Notes

PLEASE NOTE

Please note following is a list of other titles that are available in our range of Radio, Electronic and Computer books.

These should be available from all good Booksellers, Radio Component Dealers and Mail Order Companies.

However, should you experience difficulty in obtaining any title in your area, then please write directly to the publisher enclosing payment to cover the cost of the book plus adequate postage.

If you would like a complete catalogue of our entire range of Radio, Electronics and Computer Books then please send a Stamped Addressed Envelope to:

BERNARD BABANI (publishing) LTD
THE GRAMPIANS
SHEPHERDS BUSH ROAD
LONDON W6 7NF
ENGLAND

160	Coil Design and Construction Manual	£2.50
202	Handbook of Integrated Circuits (ICs) Equivalents and Substitutes	£2.95
205	Hi-Fi Loudspeaker Enclosures	£2.95
208	Practical Stereo and Quadrophony Handbook	£0.75
214	Audio Enthusiast's Handbook	£0.85
219	Solid State Novelty Projects	£0.85
220	Build Your Own Solid State Hi-Fi and Audio Accessories	£0.85
221	28 Tested Transistor Projects	£2.95
222	Solid State Short Wave Receivers for Beginners	£1.95
223	50 Projects Using IC CA3130	£1.25
224	50 CMOS IC Projects	£2.95
225	A Practical Introduction to Digital ICs	£1.75
226	How to Build Advanced Short Wave Receivers	£2.95
227	Beginners Guide to Building Electronic Projects	£1.95
228	Essential Theory for the Electronics Hobbyist	£2.50
BP1 + 14	First & Second Books of Transistor Equivalents & Substitutes	£3.50
BP2	Handbook of Radio, TV, Industrial and Transmitting Tube and Valve Equivalents	£0.60
BP6	Engineer's and Machinist's Reference Tables	£1.25
BP7	Radio and Electronic Colour Codes Data Chart	£0.95
BP27	Chart of Radio, Electronic, Semiconductor and Logic Symbols	£0.95
BP28	Resistor Selection Handbook	£0.60
BP29	Major Solid State Audio Hi-Fi Construction Projects	£0.85
BP33	Electronic Calculator Users Handbook	£1.50
BP34	Practical Repair and Renovation of Colour TVs	£2.95
BP36	50 Circuits Using Germanium Silicon and Zener Diodes	£1.50
BP37	50 Projects Using Relays, SCRs and TRIACs	£1.95
BP39	50 (FET) Field Effect Transistor Projects	£1.75
BP42	50 Simple LED Circuits	£1.95
BP44	IC 555 Projects	£2.50
BP45	Projects in Opto-electronics	£1.95
BP48	Electronic Projects for Beginners	£1.95
BP49	Popular Electronic Projects	£2.50
BP53	Practical Electronics Calculations and Formulae	£2.95
BP54	Your Electronic Calculator and Your Money	£1.35
BP56	Electronic Security Devices	£2.50
BP58	50 Circuits Using 7400 Series ICs	£2.50
BP59	Second Book of CMOS IC Projects	£1.95
BP60	Practical Construction of Pre-amps, Tone-Controls, Filters and Attenuators	£1.95
BP61	Beginners Guide to Digital Techniques	£1.95
BP62	The Simple Electronic Circuit & Components (Elements of Electronics – Book 1)	£3.50
BP63	Alternating Current Theory (Elements of Electronics – Book 2)	£3.50
BP64	Semiconductor Technology (Elements of Electronics – Book 3)	£3.50
BP65	Single IC Projects	£1.50
BP66	Beginners Guide to Microprocessors and Computing	£1.95
BP67	Counter Driver and Numeral Display Projects	£2.95
BP68	Choosing and Using Your Hi-Fi	£1.65
BP69	Electronic Games	£1.75
BP70	Transistor Radio Fault-finding Chart	£0.95
BP71	Electronic Household Projects	£1.75
BP72	A Microprocessor Primer	£1.75
BP73	Remote Control Projects	£2.50
BP74	Electronic Music Projects	£2.50
BP75	Electronic Test Equipment Construction	£1.75
BP76	Power Supply Projects	£2.50
BP77	Microprocessing Systems and Circuits (Elements of Electronics – Book 4)	£2.95
BP78	Practical Computer Experiments	£1.75
BP79	Radio Control for Beginners	£1.75
BP80	Popular Electronic Circuits – Book 1	£2.95
BP82	Electronic Projects Using Solar Cells	£1.95
BP83	VMOS Projects	£1.95
BP84	Digital IC Projects	£1.95
BP85	International Transistor Equivalents Guide	£3.50
BP86	An Introduction to BASIC Programming Techniques	£1.95
BP87	50 Simple LED Circuits – Book 2	£1.35
BP88	How to Use Op-Amps	£2.95
BP89	Communication (Elements of Electronics – Book 5)	£2.95
BP90	Audio Projects	£1.95
BP91	An Introduction to Radio DXing	£1.95
BP92	Electronics Simplified – Crystal Set Construction	£1.75
BP93	Electronic Timer Projects	£1.95
BP94	Electronic Projects for Cars and Boats	£1.95
BP95	Model Railway Projects	£1.95
BP97	IC Projects for Beginners	£1.95
BP98	Popular Electronic Circuits – Book 2	£2.25
BP99	Mini-matrix Board Projects	£1.95
BP101	How to Identify Unmarked ICs	£0.95
BP103	Multi-circuit Board Projects	£1.95
BP104	Electronic Science Projects	£2.25

BP105	Aerial Projects	£1.95
BP106	Modern Op-amp Projects	£1.95
BP107	30 Solderless Breadboard Projects – Book 1	£2.25
BP108	International Diode Equivalents Guide	£2.25
BP109	The Art of Programming the 1K ZX81	£1.95
BP110	How to Get Your Electronic Projects Working	£1.95
BP111	Audio (Elements of Electronics – Book 6)	£3.50
BP112	A Z-80 Workshop Manual	£3.50
BP113	30 Solderless Breadboard Projects – Book 2	£2.25
BP114	The Art of Programming the 16K ZX81	£2.50
BP115	The Pre-computer Book	£1.95
BP117	Practical Electronic Building Blocks – Book 1	£1.95
BP118	Practical Electronic Building Blocks – Book 2	£1.95
BP119	The Art of Programming the ZX Spectrum	£2.50
BP120	Audio Amplifier Fault-finding Chart	£0.95
BP121	How to Design and Make Your Own P.C.B.s	£1.95
BP122	Audio Amplifier Construction	£2.25
BP123	A Practical Introduction to Microprocessors	£1.95
BP124	Easy Add-on Projects for Spectrum, ZX81 & Ace	£2.75
BP125	25 Simple Amateur Band Aerials	£1.95
BP126	BASIC & PASCAL in Parallel	£1.50
BP127	How to Design Electronic Projects	£2.25
BP128	20 Programs for the ZX Spectrum and 16K ZX81	£1.95
BP129	An Introduction to Programming the ORIC-1	£1.95
BP130	Micro Interfacing Circuits – Book 1	£2.25
BP131	Micro Interfacing Circuits – Book 2	£2.25
BP132	25 Simple Shortwave Broadcast Band Aerials	£1.95
BP133	An Introduction to Programming the Dragon 32	£1.95
BP134	Easy Add-on Projects for Commodore 64, Vic-20, BBC Micro and Acorn Electron	£2.95
BP135	Secrets of the Commodore 64	£1.95
BP136	25 Simple Indoor and Window Aerials	£1.75
BP137	BASIC & FORTRAN in Parallel	£1.95
BP138	BASIC & FORTH in Parallel	£1.95
BP139	An Introduction to Programming the BBC Model B Micro	£1.95
BP140	Digital IC Equivalents and Pin Connections	£5.95
BP141	Linear IC Equivalents and Pin Connections	£5.95
BP142	An Introduction to Programming the Acorn Electron	£1.95
BP143	An Introduction to Programming the Atari 600/800 XL	£1.95
BP144	Further Practical Electronics Calculations and Formulae	£4.95
BP145	25 Simple Tropical and MW Band Aerials	£1.75
BP146	The Pre-BASIC Book	£2.95
BP147	An Introduction to 6502 Machine Code	£2.50
BP148	Computer Terminology Explained	£1.95
BP149	A Concise Introduction to the Language of BBC BASIC	£1.95
BP150	An Introduction to Programming the Sinclair QL	£1.95
BP152	An Introduction to Z80 Machine Code	£2.75
BP153	An Introduction to Programming the Amstrad CPC 464 and 664	£2.50
BP154	An Introduction to MSX BASIC	£2.50
BP155	International Radio Stations Guide	£2.95
BP156	An Introduction to QL Machine Code	£2.50
BP157	How to Write ZX Spectrum and Spectrum + Games Programs	£2.50
BP158	An Introduction to Programming the Commodore 16 and Plus 4	£2.50
BP159	How to Write Amstrad CPC 464 Games Programs	£2.50
BP161	Into the QL Archive	£2.50
BP162	Counting on QL Abacus	£2.50
BP163	Writing with QL Quill	£2.50
BP164	Drawing on QL Easel	£2.50
BP169	How to Get Your Computer Programs Running	£2.50
BP170	An Introduction to Computer Peripherals	£2.50
BP171	Easy Add-on Projects for Amstrad CPC 464, 664, 6128 and MSX Computers	£2.95
BP173	Computer Music Projects	£2.95
BP174	More Advanced Electronic Music Projects	£2.95
BP175	How to Write Word Game Programs for the Amstrad CPC 464, 664 and 6128	£2.95
BP176	A TV-DXers Handbook	£5.95
BP177	An Introduction to Computer Communications	£2.95
BP178	An Introduction to Computers in Radio	£2.95
BP179	Electronic Circuits for the Computer Control of Robots	£2.95
BP180	Computer Projects for Model Railways	£2.95
BP181	Getting the Most from Your Printer	£2.95
BP182	MIDI Projects	£2.95
BP183	An Introduction to CP/M	£2.95
BP184	An Introduction to 68000 Assembly Language	£2.95
BP185	Electronic Synthesiser Construction	£2.95
BP186	Walkie-Talkie Projects	£2.95
BP187	A Practical Reference Guide to Word Processing on the Amstrad PCW 8256 and PCW 8512	£5.95
BP188	Getting Started with BASIC and LOGO on the Amstrad PCW 8256 and PCW 8512	£6.95
BP189	Using Your Amstrad CPC Disc Drives	£2.95
BP190	More Advanced Electronic Security Projects	£2.95
BP191	Simple Applications of the Amstrad CPCs for Writers	£2.95
BP192	More Advanced Power Supply Projects	£2.95
BP193	Starting LOGO	£2.95
BP194	Modern Opto Device Projects	£2.95
BP195	An Introduction to Communications and Direct Broadcast Satellites	£3.95
BP196	BASIC & LOGO in Parallel	£2.95